Healthy Mexican
Cook Book

JACQUELINE HIGUERA MCMAHAN

The Olive Press

COVER DESIGN: ROBERT MCMAHAN
BOOK DESIGN : ROBERT MCMAHAN

Published by Olive Press
P.O. Box 194, Lake Hughes, CA 93532

Library of Congress Catalogue Number 94-069176
ISBN: 1-881656-04-7

Printed and bound in the United States of America

The recipes in this book have been nutritionally analyzed
by Hill Nutrition Associates, Inc. My thanks go to Lynne
and Bill Hill for excellent work and understanding.

TO DAD,
WHO HAS ALWAYS BEEN A PROPONET OF GOOD NUTRITION
ACCOMPANIED BY ICE CREAM

OTHER BOOKS BY JACQUELINE HIGUERA MCMAHAN
CALIFORNIA RANCHO COOKING,1983
THE SALSA BOOK, 1986
THE RED AND GREEN CHILE BOOK, 1988
THE HEALTHY FIESTA, 1990
THE MEXICAN BREAKFAST BOOK, 1992
THE CHIPOTLE CHILE COOKBOOK, 1994

Contents

INTRODUCTION III

CHAPTER I HEALTHY MEXICAN 13

THE BEST BEANS 16

THICKENED BEANS 16

ARROZ NEGRO 17

GRANDMA'S RICE WITH EMBELLISHMENT 18

CHILES RELLENOS 19

MARINATED CHILES RELLENOS 21

CREAM CHEESE FILLING 22

QUICK FRESH SALSA 23

POBLANO CHILES STUFFED WITH FRUIT AND CHICKEN 23

CHILES STUFFED WITH CORN AND ZUCCHINI 25

SPEEDY 30 MINUTE POZOLE VEGETABLE SOUP 26

SPEAKING OF ENCHILADAS 27

RED CHILE AND ROASTED GARLIC SAUCE 28

STACKED ONION AND CHEESE ENCHILADAS 29

TURKEY BREAST CHORIZO 30

JOSE'S SPECIAL 32

HEALTHY FLOUR TORTILLAS 33

SALSA CHICKEN 35

CHAPTER II SALADS **37**
TURKEY CHIPOTLE TOSTADA 40
PICKLED PINK ONIONS 41
CHICKEN TOSTADA WITH GRAPE SALSA 42
THE BEST CHICKEN TOSTADA SALAD WITH CREAMY MEX DRESSING 43
BLACK BEANS FOR SALADS AND TOSTADAS 45
TACO SALAD WITH SALSA DRESSING 46
JALAPEÑO CARROTS 48
GUACAMOLE DRESSING 49
THE CAPTAIN'S CAESAR SALAD 49
WARM SPAGHETTI SALAD WITH SALSA 52
JICAMA AND RED PEPPER SALAD 54
BASQUE SALAD 55
PEAR SALAD 56
GRAPEFRUIT, ORANGE, AND AVOCADO SALAD WITH TEXAS DRESSING 57
RED CABBAGE AND APPLE SALAD WITH POPPY SEED DRESSING 58
MEXICAN COLE SLAW 59
NEW MEXICAN POTATO SALAD 60
RED PEPPER CILANTRO PESTO TORTE 61
MARINATED JICAMA STICKS 63
SKINNY GUACAMOLE 64
BLACK BEAN DIP 65
TORTILLA TURKEY ROLL-UPS 66
CHAPTER III SOPAS **69**
THE SOUPS OF MEXICO 69
FEARLESS CHICKEN BROTH 71
FRIENDLY CHICKEN BROTH 72
JANET BLANDINO REDMAN'S DOORSTEP CHICKEN SOUP 74
SOPA DE LIMA 76
MEXICAN MINESTRONE WITH CILANTRO PESTO 78
CILANTRO PESTO 80
SOPA DE FIDEOS ANGEL HAIR PASTA SOUP 81
ME AND HUGO'S CALDO DE TLALPEÑO 82
YELLOW RICE 84
ENCHILADA SOUP 84
SPICY SPLIT PEA SOUP 87
SWEET POTATO AND JALAPEÑO SOUP 88
TOASTED SOPA DE TORTILLA 90
MEXICAN VEGETABLE SALSA SOUP 92
ALBÓNDIGAS FOR SOUP 93
TARASCAN BEAN SOUP 94
BLACK BEAN SOUP WITH MARINATED RICE 96

EASY MEXICAN GAZPACHO 98
SOPA DE MAÍZ 100
CHAPTER IV MEXICAN SEAFOOD **103**
GRILLED YUCATÁN FISH 105
BAJA CALIFORNIA FISH TACOS 106
LUCY'S HOT SALSA 107
JALAPEÑO LIME SALSA 108
MEXICAN CEVICHE SALAD 109
RED SNAPPER FILETS VERACRUZ STYLE 110
MICHAEL GRANT'S BOUILLABAISSE CHILI 112
BLACK BEAN SEAFOOD CHILI 114
CHAPTER V THE HOLY TRINITY **117**
DYNAMITE VEGETARIAN CHILI 119
BASIC SIMPLE BEANS AS A FOUNDATION FOR RECIPES 121
BLACK BEAN CHILI AU GRATIN 122
BLACK BEAN PANCAKES 124
NAVAHO BEAN SALAD 126
LENTIL CHILI 128
WHITE BEAN CHILI 129
CORN, THE SECOND FOOD OF THE TRINITY **131**
POSOLE 133
THE TAMALE PIE 136
RANCHO COLACHE 138
CORN-BROWN RICE-LENTIL SALAD WITH JALAPEÑO VINAIGRETTE 139
JALAPEÑO VINAIGRETTE 141
CORN ENCHILADAS 142
GREEN CORN TAMALES 144
PAN DE MAÍZ 146
CHICKEN CHILI 147
BLUE CORN BANANA MUFFINS 149
CHILES, THE APEX OF THE TRINITY **151**
GREEN CHILE STEW 152
TURKEY BREAST GREEN CHILE STEW 155
SANTA FE STROGANOFF 156
VEGETABLE BURRITOS WITH KILLER RED SAUCE 158
KILLER RED SAUCE 159
CHICKEN COLORADO 161
ENCHILADAS OF THE JARDÍN 162
EGGPLANT ENCHILADAS 164
ENCHILADAS VERDES 165
FAST TOMATILLO SALSA 167

SPICY TURKEY TENDERLOINS WITH RED PEPPER SAUCE 168
CHICKEN RÁPIDO.. 170
SOFT TACOS WITH SALSAS 171
HACKED-UP SALSA 172
JACQUIE'S EVERYDAY SALSA 172
INSIDE-OUT QUESADILLA WITH SMOKED FIRE 173
SMOKED FIRE 175
CHAPTER VI LICUADOS **177**
SAN MIGUEL MARKET LICUADO 178
FRUIT RAINBOW LICUADO 178
NUTTY PINEAPPLE SHAKE 179
STRAWBERRIES AND CREAM LICUADO 180
STRAWBERRY ORANGE LICUADO 180
AGUA FRESA DE SANDÍA WATERMELON JUICE 181
JAMAICA 183
CHAPTER VII INDULGENCES **185**
POACHED PEARS WITH AMARETTI FILLING 187
APPLE BLUEBERRY CRISP 189
STRAWBERRY MERINGUE SHORTCAKES 190
STRAWBERRY BROWNIE PIZZA 192
DEVILISH ANGEL FOOD 193
INNOCENT CHOCOLATE SOUFFLE 195
NORMA'S ELEGANT PERSIMMON 196
FRESH FRUIT IN VANILLA SYRUP 197
INDEX 198
RESOURCES 206

INTRODUCTION

To be inspired by the healthfulness of Mexican foods, look toward the varied native cuisines, found in the different regions of this vast country, and their blend of Indian and European. There you will find the key.

European tastes introduced by the conquistadores in the sixteenth century melded with Indian tastes, such as the fine palates of the Aztecs. Looking at Mexican food from this angle, you can only be impressed by the earthiness and healthfulness of the daily diet which amazingly resembles the highly touted Mediterrean diet only with corn tortillas and chiles thrown in.

As Sybille Bedford observed over forty years ago in *A Sudden View, A Mexican Journey*, "Certain styles of cooking run like a thread across the globe, and certain folk themes appear over and over again at places unrelated to each other. The cooking of Mexico belongs by ingredients and technique loosely to the European Mediterranean. The new food was a graft that took well. It suited the climate, the potentialities of the land, and joined quite naturally with the indigenous roots ..... returning full eclectic circle, herb to herb and oil to olive."

The real heart and soul of Mexican food is healthy. It's just been bastardized in the translation. A thousand light years away is the 1,600 calorie chimichanga which gets a thumbs down for its nutritional benefits. Now we just have to reconnect to the real Mexican food or to a new interpretation of the old.

HEALTHY MEXICAN PYRAMID OF FOODS

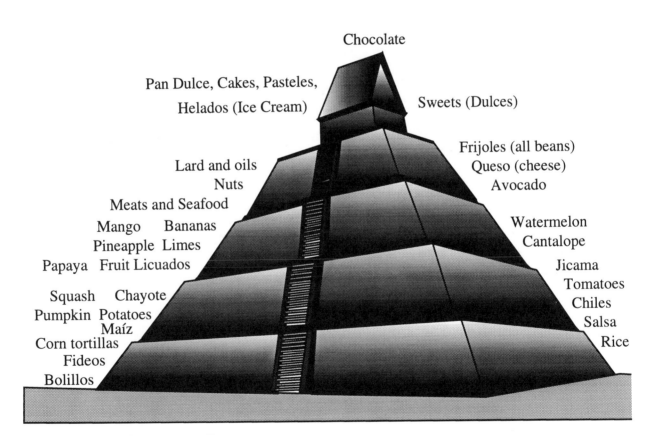

Chocolate

Pan Dulce, Cakes, Pasteles,
Helados (Ice Cream)

Sweets (Dulces)

Frijoles (all beans)
Queso (cheese)
Avocado

Lard and oils
Nuts

Meats and Seafood

Mango   Bananas
Pineapple Limes
Papaya Fruit Licuados

Watermelon
Cantalope

Jicama
Tomatoes
Chiles
Salsa
Rice

Squash   Chayote
Pumpkin Potatoes
Maíz
Corn tortillas
Fideos
Bolillos

HEALTHY MEXICAN

CHAPTER I

TRADITIONAL MEXICAN DISHES, LIGHTENED AND ENLIGHTENED

Recently, much furor has been raised over the unhealthiness of certain Mexican dishes like the fried chimichangas, refried beans, fried chiles rellenos, and fried tacos. These foods, as dearly beloved as they are to some devotees, are not truly representative of Mexican food just as fastfood pizza is not representative of Italian cuisine.

The Mexican pyramid of foods has a foundation of corn-related recipes made with ground maíz such as tortillas and tamales. Vegetables such as squash, pumpkin, tomatoes, garlic, chile peppers, chayote, and greens make up the middle of the pyramid. Small amounts of meat, except for feasts and fiestas, are eaten for protein but beans (combined with other starches to make a complete protein) are the star, eaten in great amounts. Cheeses, such as fresh goat cheese and the lower-fat, crumbly queso ranchero are appreciated in small amounts on top of enchiladas and dishes of beans. The Mexicans consume a great number of exotic fruits such as mango, papaya, many types of bananas, and pineapple. You will often see fruit vendors doing a brisk business with their fresh fruit slices splashed with lime and chile powder. If that is not enough fruit, they sip licuados of pureed fruits for refreshment.

The biggest criticism of the Mexican diet could be directed at sugar. They do love their refrescos such as the ubiquitous Coka. Panaderías in every city and small village serve forth endless pan dulce. Hopefully, most Mexicans consume greater amounts of the other foods of the pyramid, balancing out the sweets.

Within this chapter, I take a different approach to the traditional Mexican favorites. Some Mexican classics like chiles rellenos are under the greatest fat attack. Within this book, I am just enlightening and lightening traditional dishes, not taking away from their charm. After all it should not be like having water for chocolate.

When I think of Mexican food, I think of beans or frijoles. Of course I love beans and I could happily make entire meals out of delicious beans, tortillas, and salsa. Rather than just boil beans, I like to put flavorful ingredients into the pot-tons of garlic and whole chiles.

It has been discovered that beans do not have to be soaked. Soaking only shortens cooking time and really doesn't remarkably increase digestibility. If you eat beans regularly, you will have little trouble digesting them. The more beans you eat, the better it gets.

My grandmother, who probably cooked a pot of beans every other day of her life, was the queen of bean cookery. She told me that she never soaked beans because it took away flavor. I didn't believe her for about 30 years. Now I believe her. I kept following all of those cautionary tales about soaking beans overnight or quick soaking them in boiling water for 4 hours. The beans still took over 2 hours to cook. Now I thoroughly rinse the beans and check for little rocks and put them to cook covered in plenty of fresh water. Unsoaked beans do require more water. They still take 2 hours to cook but they taste more wonderful.

THE BEST BEANS

These beans require no sautéing of ingredients and you can replace all chiles with the chipotle chiles. Their smokiness makes it seem as though you have added wood-smoked bacon.

PER SERVING:
276 calories
17 g protein
51 g carbohydrate
1 g fat
0 mg cholesterol
858 mg sodium

1 pound pink, pinto, or black beans
10 cups water
2 dried red chiles (California, New Mexican, or ancho
  or 2 dried chipotle chiles
1 tablespoon minced garlic (3 to 4 cloves)
1 cup chopped onion
2 to 3 teaspoons salt, added after 1 hour

Hint: keep hot water available in tea kettle to add to beans if necessary. Beans should be submerged in liquid at all times.

Place beans in colander or strainer and rinse under running water. Check well for small stones. Place in large 5 quart pot so the beans can happily simmer without boiling over. Add the water, dried chiles, garlic, and onion. Bring beans to a simmer and then keep on medium low heat for 2 to 2 and 1/2 hours. Add salt toward the end of the cooking time.

Serves 6, 1 cup portions.

THICKENED BEANS

PER SERVING:
153 calories
8 g protein
25 g carbohydrate
2 g fat
0 mg cholesterol
429 mg sodium

These come awfully close to refried beans except they aren't fried, they're simmered in a open, wide skillet while you mash. The simmering and the mashing makes them thicken nicely.

Cooking spray, olive oil or canola oil
2 teaspoons oil
3 cups of cooked beans with liquid

Spray a heavy nonstick 10-inch skillet with cooking spray, turn heat on medium, and add rest of oil. When hot, add 1 cup of beans with some of liquid. Use bean masher or wide spoon to mash beans until very creamy. Once beans are creamy, add the rest and keep mashing until beans are thick enough and look like refries. This method works well with pinto, pink, anasazi, and black beans.

Serves 6, 1/2 cup portions.

ARROZ NEGRO

PER SERVING:
211 calories
5 g protein
43 g carbohydrate
2 g fat
0 mg cholesterol
394 mg sodium

Black rice is one of those delicious surprises that results when you have extra bean juice in the pot and you need somewhere to put it. If you plan on making Arroz Negro, add at least 1 cup more water to the bean pot.

Olive oil cooking spray

1 teaspoon olive oil
1/4 cup chopped onion
1 clove garlic
1 cup long-grain white rice
2 tablespoons tomato paste
2 cups black bean juice from cooking pot (include 2
    tablespoons black beans)
1/2 teaspoon salt

Generously spray bottom of 2-quart pot with lid. Add olive oil and heat pot. Add onion, garlic, and rice and sauté until golden, about 3 to 4 minutes.

Then add tomato paste, black bean pot juices, and salt. Bring to a simmer, place on lid, and cook over low heat for 25 minutes.

Serves 4,

GRANDMA'S RICE WITH EMBELLISHMENT

PER SERVING:
157 calories
3 g protein
30 g carbohydrate
3 g fat
0 mg cholesterol
218 mg sodium

When you are serving spicy main dishes Grandma's rice is a perfect accompaniment. Grandma fried her rice in a lot more olive oil to give it the toasted flavor typical of Spanish rice.

1 tablespoon olive oil
1 cup long-grain rice
1/2 cup chopped onion
1 teaspoon minced garlic
1/2 cup skinned, chopped tomato
2 and 1/2 cups water
1/2 teaspoon salt
2 teaspoons ground chile
1/2 cup chopped carrots (about 2)
1/2 cup petite frozen peas

Heat the olive oil in a deep 2-quart pot with a lid. Sauté the rice until it gives off a whiff of a popcorn smell and is a little golden. Add the chopped onion and sauté for a couple of minutes, mixing it into the rice. Add the garlic and chopped tomato and sauté.

Add the water, salt, and ground chile. Simmer until little holes start to appear in the surface of the rice, about 10 minutes. Sprinkle the chopped carrots on top along with the peas. Put on the lid.

Cook the rice on low heat for 10 more minutes. Then turn off the heat and leave undisturbed for 10 more minutes.

6 servings.

CHILES RELLENOS

Relleno is the Spanish word for stuffed and stuffed chiles are real carriers of fat if they are the ones filled with rich cheese, dipped in an egg batter, and fried. There is a way to make them which tastes equally as good and that is to fill them with chicken, corn, or black beans and maybe a little reduced-fat cheese. But the ultimate technique, our favorite, is to dip them in egg white and then roll them in wonderfully seasoned French bread crumbs. These chiles are crusty, golden wonders which you will like better than the fatty ones or just as well!

8 Anaheim or New Mexican green chiles (mild to hot), charred, carefully peeled and seeds removed
4 ounces grated reduced-fat Monterey Jack or Cheddar cheese
1/2 cup all-purpose flour
3 egg whites
4 cups fluffy bread crumbs made from Italian or French bread
1/4 cup finely ground Parmesan cheese
1 and 1/2 teaspoons oregano
1 teaspoon chile powder
Olive oil or canola oil mist
1 tablespoon melted butter

PER SERVING:
334 calories
19 g protein
38 g carbohydrate
11 g fat
32 mg cholesterol
588 mg sodium

First make your bread crumbs by placing bread into the bowl of a food processor. Process until you have a fluffy texture. Add the Parmesan cheese, oregano, and chile powder to the bread crumbs. Place this mixture on a piece of waxed paper.

Carefully slit each charred and peeled green chile along one side so that you can stuff in about 1/2 ounce grated cheese. Press down on the chile with the flat of your hand to seal the cheese inside.

Dust each chile with flour. I like to do this on a piece of wax paper.

Beat the egg whites just until they are very liquid. Holding both ends of each chile, dip in the egg white just to coat.

Place the chile on top of the bread crumbs and sprinkle more crumbs on top of chile, pressing them so that they adhere.

Place prepared chile relleno on a nonstick baking sheet that you have sprayed with canola oil. When you have completed the preparation of all the chiles, drizzle the melted butter on top. Bake in a preheated 375 degree oven for about 20 minutes or until the chiles are golden.

Serves 4 to 6 (most people eat 2 chiles rellenos)

MARINATED CHILES RELLENOS

Jan Dominguez charmingly relates in her *Sandwich Cuisine* cookbook how her family and friends love her stuffed chiles so much, they refer to them just as "The Chiles." I brought these once to a summer picnic before a play at the John Ford Theater in Los Angeles. There wasn't a scrap left.

Below is my adaptation of Jan's recipe.

8 Anaheim or mild New Mexican red or green chiles
1 and 1/2 cups white wine vinegar
1/2 cup rice vinegar (unseasoned)
1 cup water
1 tablespoon olive oil
1 tablespoon crushed cumin seeds
2 crushed garlic cloves
2 teaspoons sugar
1 teaspoon salt
1 bay leaf
1 teaspoon oregano
1 carrot, peeled
Cream cheese filling (see recipe below)
2 cups fresh homemade or store-bought red salsa
1 cup grated reduced-fat Monterey Jack cheese

First prepare chiles so that they may be marinating while you do the rest. Char chiles over flame or grill until they are blackened. Place in paper bag to steam for 10 minutes. This will help loosen the skin. Gently slip off skins being careful not to tear chile. Cut a lengthwise slit carefully down the side of each chile. Remove seeds., Set chiles aside while you prepare the marinade.

PER SERVING:
278 calories
17 g protein
21 g carbohydrate
16 g fat
50 mg cholesterol
853 mg sodium

The marinade gives added flavor to the chiles and allows the cook the delete the frying usually called for with chiles rellenos. In a saucepan, combine wine vinegar, rice vinegar, water, oil, cumin seeds, garlic, sugar, salt, and herbs. Simmer for 10 minutes; remove from heat and pour into large bowl. Add carrot (to be marinated and chopped later for the cream cheese filling). Add the chiles and marinate for 2 to 4 hours.

When ready to serve, drain chiles from marinade and stuff with about 2 tablespoons of the cream cheese mixture. Lay out in a baking pan. Spoon a couple of tablespoons of salsa over the top of each chile and sprinkle each one with a little grated cheese. Place chiles 8 inches under medium hot broiler until cheese is melted.

You can reduce fat further by not including grated cheese topping.

Serves 4 because each person will eat 2 chiles.

CREAM CHEESE FILLING

8 ounces reduced-fat cream cheese, softened
2 green onion, minced
1/4 cup cilantro, minced
1 jalapeño chile, seeded and minced
1 marinated carrot, minced

Combine cream cheese, green onion, cilantro, jalapeño, and carrot. Use as stuffing for marinated chiles.

Makes enough filling for 8 chiles.

QUICK FRESH SALSA

3 cups seeded, diced tomatoes
1/4 cup diced red onion
2 minced cloves garlic
1 to 2 jalapeño chiles, seeded and minced
1 to 2 tablespoons marinade left from chiles
1/2 teaspoon salt

Combine all ingredients; mix well. Use any time you need a basic quick salsa or spoon over the tops of the chiles rellenos above. Makes about 3 and 1/2 cups salsa.

POBLANO CHILES STUFFED WITH FRUIT AND CHICKEN

A version of this recipe, an adaptation of traditional chiles en nogada, is served by Zarela Martinez at her New York restaurant.

8 large poblano chiles or Anaheim chiles
1 tablespoon olive oil
1 cup chopped onion
1 whole chicken breast, boned, skinned, finely diced
1/2 cup chicken broth, reduced sodium or homemade
1/2 cup diced dried apricots, soaked in hot water
1/4 cup golden raisins, blanched in hot water
1/2 teaspoon salt
1/2 teaspoon cinnamon
pinch of ground cloves

PER SERVING:
209 calories
17 g protein
29 g carbohydrate
5 g fat
22 mg cholesterol
411 mg sodium

1/2 cup diced, peeled peach
Walnut Sauce
1 8-ounce package fat-free cream cheese
1/3 cup 1% milk
1/4 cup toasted walnuts
1 pomegranate, red seeds removed for garnish

Char the poblano chiles over a flame, under a broiler, or over a grill until surface of chiles are blackened. Place in paper bag for 10 minutes to steam and loosen skins. Then peel off skins and gently cut a slit along the side of each chile. Pull out the thick seed pod right under the stem of the chile.

Heat the oil in a nonstick skillet and sauté onion for 5 minutes until softened and then push aside and add minced chicken. Sauté for about 6 minutes and then add the broth, drained dried fruit, salt, cinnamon, and cloves. Simmer over medium high heat . Remove pan from heat and stir in diced peaches.

For the sauce, place cream cheese and milk into bowl and whisk until smooth and of sauce consistency. Add the nuts.

All of the above steps may be completed hours before serving. When you are ready, stuff the chiles with the fruit-chicken mixture. Place on an oiled baking dish. Pour cream cheese sauce over tops of chiles. Heat in a preheated 350 degree oven for 8 minutes. Remove chiles to a serving platter or individual plates. Scatter a couple of teaspoons pomegranate seeds on top of each chile.

Serves 8.

CHILES STUFFED WITH CORN AND ZUCCHINI

These chiles rellenos are a celebration of all that is available in summer. Since nothing is fried, again you can enjoy these without guilt!

8 large poblano or Anaheim green chiles, charred
2 teaspoons olive oil
1/4 cup minced onion
2 cloves minced garlic
1/2 cup corn kernels (fresh or frozen)
1 tablespoon minced epazote or cilantro
1/2 teaspoon salt
2 zucchini (1/2 pound), cut into 1/4-inch dice
1/2 cup grated reduced-fat Cheddar cheese

Heat olive oil in a medium nonstick skillet and fry onion until softened, about 3 minutes. Add the minced garlic during the last minute. Stir in the corn, epazote, salt, and diced zucchini, continuing to cook for another 5 minutes. Remove from heat and add the cheese.

Remove charred skin from chiles and cut a slit down the side of each chile. Rinse out the seeds. Place about 2 tablespoons zucchini-corn mixture inside each chile. Place filled chiles on an oiled baking sheet and heat in a preheated 375 degree oven for about 8 minutes. The chiles just need warming.

Serves 8.

PER SERVING:
93 calories
5 g protein
14 g carbohydrate
3 g fat
5 mg cholesterol
197 mg sodium

SPEEDY 30 MINUTE POZOLE VEGETABLE SOUP

PER SERVING:
395 calories
35 g protein
42 g carbohydrate
10 g fat
82 mg cholesterol
1200 mg sodium

I know that there are cold evenings when you need something warming but you don't have the energy or time for a big production. Stop at the store on your way home and buy some convenience items to make your cooking easier. In California there are Mexican fast food places with grilled chicken, marinated in fruit juices, which is great to shred for quick tostada salads, soft tacos, enchiladas, or Speedy 30 Minute Pozole Soup. If you don't have a Mexican chicken place nearby, purchase a rotisserie chicken from the supermarket.

1 quart fat-free chicken broth, canned or homemade
2 15 -ounce cans golden hominy, drained
1/2 cup diced onion
2 teaspoons minced garlic
1 teaspoon dried oregano
1 teaspoon crushed cumin
2 teaspoons ground red chile powder
2 whole dried red chiles, preferably ancho (optional)
*Half of 1 cooked chicken (about 1 and 1/2 pounds
    including bones)*
1 zucchini, trimmed and diced
2 carrots, peeled and cut into 2-inch pieces
1/4 cup minced cilantro
2 fresh limes

Note: analysis is for reduced-sodium fat free broth. Reduce sodium further by rinsing hominy.

Pull the chicken off the bones, discarding the skin. Cut chicken into 1-inch chunks.

In a 3-quart pot, simmer the broth, hominy, onion, garlic, oregano, cumin, and red chile powder 20 minutes. If you have whole red dried chiles, add here also as it provides great flavor.

This will give you enough time to pull the chicken off the bones and cut into chunks, prepare the zucchini, carrots, and cilantro. Add the vegetables and chicken to the pozole and simmer for just 15 more minutes. Stir in the cilantro just before serving so it remains bright green Each person squeezes 1/2 lime over his soup before eating. Serves 4.

SPEAKING OF ENCHILADAS

The best of two worlds is combined in the following enchilada recipe, page 29. Enchiladas are stacked in New Mexico and in old Mexico, enchiladas are never baked into oblivion. The enchiladas here are stacked and served. No baking required.

You can really be creative with fillings because you don't have to worry about trying to cram them into a tube shape. You stack the softened and sauced tortillas between the filling and cheese. Watch those native New Mexicans. They frequently call for a fried egg on top of the stack.

I make up the enchilada sauce in advance. Then I can come home and put together enchiladas in 20 minutes. What's wonderful about this sauce is that it is thick and unctuous due to the chiles and vegetables. Traditional enchilada sauces are usually thickened with shortening, lard, flour, or cornstarch. You can use the Red Chile And Roasted Garlic Sauce as a base for many dishes besides enchiladas. It's good poured over Vegetarian Burritos or added to soups and stews. It makes plain vegetable soup come alive.

RED CHILE AND ROASTED GARLIC SAUCE

PER SERVING
1/2 cup sauce:
46 calories
2 g protein
9 g carbohydrate
1 g fat
0 mg cholesterol
283 mg sodium

First prepare the sauce:
1 head of garlic, top cut off
1 teaspoon olive oil
1 sprig thyme
1/2 large onion
8 large California or New Mexican dried red chiles
1 chipotle chile (dried or canned in adobo sauce)
Soaking water to cover chiles
3 cups water for cooking chiles and tomatoes
8 ounces ripe tomatoes
1 tablespoon New Mexican red chile powder
    (optional)
1 teaspoon salt
1 teaspoon crushed cumin seeds
1 teaspoon cider vinegar

Before you begin anything else, place head of garlic and onion in middle of large square of aluminum foil. Drizzle olive oil on garlic, place sprig of thyme on top and wrap up the entire package of the garlic, thyme, and onion. Bake for 1 hour at 375 degrees.

Meanwhile, pour boiling water over the red chiles, adding the chipotle chile only if you are using a dried one. Let the chiles soak while the garlic is baking.

Place 3 cups fresh water into a 3-quart pot, adding the

soaked red chiles, the chipotle, the head of garlic, thyme, onion, and tomatoes. Simmer for 45 minutes. Then working in batches, use blender to puree the soaked, stemmed chiles, all of the garlic cloves removed from the entire head, onion, and tomatoes. Push this puree through a strainer back into the pot (just to remove all the tomato and chile skins).

Taste the red chile sauce and if it isn't picante enough, add the optional red chile powder. Also add the salt, cumin, and vinegar. Simmer the sauce for 15 minutes to thicken.

Makes about 1 quart sauce which will keep for 2 weeks refrigerated.

STACKED ONION AND CHEESE ENCHILADAS

Canola oil or olive oil spray
2 teaspoons canola oil, divided
4 corn tortillas
1/2 cup diced mild onions
1 cup reduced-fat Monterey Jack cheese
1 and 1/2 cups Roasted Garlic and Red Chile Sauce

Preheat oven to 250 degrees.

PER SERVING:
399 calories
21 g protein
41 g carbohydrate
18 g fat
40 mg cholesterol
866 mg sodium

Spray a large nonstick 12-inch skillet with canola oil or olive oil mist. Add 1 teaspoon canola oil and heat skillet. Have the sauce heating in a wide skillet also. The chopped onion and grated cheese should be ready and waiting. Heatproof dinner plates should be ready and waiting and your guest better be there too—standing by or don't invite him again unless he is your husband.

Note: for a milder sauce use all California dried red chiles and no chipotles.

Fry two corn tortillas at a time in the hot skillet. Give them at least a minute on each side. Using tongs, dip one tortilla at a time into the heated sauce. Place the sauced tortilla onto the plate. Sprinkle with 1/4 cup cheese and 1/4 cup onion. Dip the second tortilla and stack on top of the cheese and onions. Sprinkle with another 1/4 cup cheese. Place in the warm oven. Hold there just until you prepare the next stacked enchilada in the same manner.

Serves 2. Recipe easily doubles or triples.

TURKEY BREAST CHORIZO

PER SERVING:
Per 1 oz portion
46 calories
7 g protein
1 g carbohydrate
2 g fat
18 mg cholesterol
171 mg sodium

Chorizo is one of our favorites treats when cooked with eggs for a Sunday morning but we have had to keep it for special treats and find a lower-calorie way to enjoy it. The ground turkey breast keeps the chorizo much lower in fat, using the prepared sausage to hold everything together as a flavorful binder.

Bob Harris, one of my loyal reader-cooks with whom I mutually share many ideas, gave me the hint of adding the jalapeño juice (from the canned and pickled jalapeños) as a seasoning for chile sauces. I especially like using it for the chorizo . Cheryl and Bill Jamison feature a great recipe for Chipotle Chorizo in their *Texas Home Cooking* (Harvard Common Press) which gave me the idea for the chipotle.

This chorizo is so good you don't know you're supposed to be missing something.

1 and 1/4 pounds ground all-white meat turkey breast
6 ounces extra lean turkey-pork prepared sausage
2 tablespoon ground red chile powder, preferably New Mexican
2 to 3 tablespoons pureed chipotle en adobo
1/4 cup apple cider vinegar or juice from pickled jalapeños
1 tablespoon minced garlic
1 tablespoon dried oregano
1 teaspoon ground cumin
1 teaspoon salt

Mix the ground turkey and prepared sausage with all of the above seasonings. Work chorizo together with your hands. Keeps well for three days if well-wrapped. If you do not plan on using it all for one recipe, seal the chorizo with plastic wrap in quarter pound packages and freeze.

JOSE'S SPECIAL

PER SERVING:
171 calories
22 g protein
7 g carbohydrate
6 g fat
143 mg cholesterol
474 mg sodium

Many years ago in San Francisco, "Joe's Special" was a famous concoction of fried hamburger, onions, eggs, and fresh spinach. It was the kind of nourishment we ate at 2 AM when we were young and hungry and had just slinked out of a dim, smoky North Beach jazz club.

Even though that kind of youth is now a memory, my husband and I still hunger for Joe's Special which has evolved into Jose's because the hamburger is replaced with Turkey Chorizo. The spiciness fills up the void left by the lack of grease. It makes a marvelous, simple Sunday night supper especially when we can pull the little packages of chorizo out of the freezer.

Olive oil or canola oil spray
1/2 pound Turkey Chorizo
1/4 cup minced onion
1/2 pound fresh spinach, washed well and chopped
4 egg whites
2 eggs
4 warm and soft corn tortillas

Note: you can use all whole eggs if you are young and foolish and haven't started considering mortality.

Spray a nonstick 12-inch skillet with olive oil. Fry the Turkey Chorizo and onion for about 10 minutes over medium heat. Next stir in the spinach and continue frying until wilted, about 3 minutes.

Beat the egg whites and eggs together just until well-blended. Pour them over the chorizo and spinach. Stir until the whole thing is one big wonderful scrambled mess which will happen in about 5 minutes. Eat immediately. Serves 4 for a light midnight breakfast.

HEALTHY FLOUR TORTILLAS

These are good any time, even just toasted for breakfast. They are especially good to wrap up Jose's Special or some Thickened Beans, page 16.

The wonder of these tortillas is that they are just as flaky as my Grandmother's traditional. I am grateful to the testing kitchens of Eating Well magazine for discovering the trick of freezing part of the flour and oil so that the mixture simulates vegetable shortening.

4 cups unbleached all-purpose flour
1/2 teaspoon baking powder
4 tablespoons canola oil
1 and 1/2 teaspoons salt
1 and 1/2 cups warm water

Sift flour and baking powder together. Remove 1/2 cup of mixture and blend canola oil into it using a fork. Cover tightly with plastic wrap and freeze 1 to 2 hours.

Use a large blending fork to mix the cold flour-oil mixture (taken directly from the freezer) into the dry flour mixture until resembles pastry crumbs. Mix the salt into the warm water. Drizzle over flour; blend. Mold into a soft ball of dough. Knead dough for 1 minute right in the bowl. Cover bowl with plastic wrap and let dough rest for 30 minutes to 2 hours at room temperature.

Oil a jelly roll pan. Form dough into 14 balls. Flatten balls into 3-inch rounds. Let them rest for 30 minutes,

PER SERVING:
157 calories
4 g protein
27 g carbohydrate
4 g fat
0 mg cholesterol
211 mg sodium

covered in plastic wrap so they don't dry out. Resting not only mellows the dough but relaxes it, making it easier to roll into tortillas.

Preheat a griddle or comal. Dust floured board and place a tortilla round in center. Roll into larger circle, rolling from center outwards. Make a quarter turn of the tortilla after each two strokes. This will keep the tortilla round instead of being shaped like a violin. The perfect rolling pin is a wooden dowel or sawed-off, clean broom handle.

Roll your tortilla to an 8-inch circle. Use your fingers to stretch it to a 10-inch circle. Hold the tortilla on top of one palm while you draw fingers of the other hand underneath the tortilla, stretching it.

Place tortilla on preheated griddle. Turn over 10 seconds until light brown freckles form and tortilla puffs in spots. Turn four or 5 times. When tortilla stops puffing, it is done. Makes 12 to 14 flour tortillas

SALSA CHICKEN

A simple, savory recipe that is too well-loved to leave out.

6 boneless, skinned chicken breast filets
16 ounces thick and chunky salsa, bottled okay
5 cups fluffy breadcrumbs from Italian or French
    bread
2 cloves garlic
1 teaspoon oregano
1/2 teaspoon salt
1 teaspoon ground red chile
Olive oil or canola oil mist
2 tablespoons butter

Marinate chicken in salsa for at least one hour.

Grind your fluffy breadcrumbs (from day-old bread) in a food processor, adding the garlic, oregano, salt and, ground chile. Place on large piece of waxed paper.

Remove chicken from salsa, keeping as many little chunks as you can. Press chicken onto the crumbs. Press more crumbs on top of filets.

Spray nonstick baking sheet with oil. Lay out the chicken. Drizzle with butter. Bake in 375 degree oven for 30 to 35 minutes. If you want chicken browned, you can place under broiler for a minute. Serves 6.

PER SERVING:
256 calories
30 g protein
18 g carbohydrate
6 g fat
79 mg cholesterol
769 mg sodium

This is a case where bottled chunky salsa is better than fresh salsa which can exude more water.

SALADS

CHAPTER II

TRADITIONAL, NON TRADITIONAL, AND APPETIZERS

side from being health conscious or calorie conscious, most of us love a beautiful salad. It can be appealing to the eye and satisfy our primitive need for something to chew on. But at home, making salad is regretfully a neglected art form. Many cooks expend their energy on the main dish or company dessert, leaving the salad to be thrown together at the last minute (with bottled dressing). A salad can serve as an entire lunch or dinner if it contains bits of protein, vegetables, pasta, beans, homemade croutons or tortilla chips.

Tricks for Making Great Salads
That Are High In Flavor and Lower In Fat

A great salad deserves a great dressing. Even a tostada salad, which can be one of the highest-fat plates in a Mexican restaurant, can have its calories cut in half by making it with lower fat dressing (and cutting out the sour cream and guacamole!).

DECREASE THE OIL IN YOUR DRESSINGS AND EXCHANGE THEM FOR OTHER FLAVORFUL IN-GREDIENTS.

Dressings are the culprits. They can carry most of the fat calories. The trick is to use flavorful dressings that carry maximum flavor in minimum amounts. I have not yet found a bottled nonfat dressing that doesn't taste fake but I have found a way to lower the amount of oil needed in homemade dressings by adding Dijon mustard, which is a great natural emulsifier, rice vinegar, balsamic vinegar, wine, broth, and yogurt. The dressing can be thickened by pureeing with garlic, shallots, onions, a tomato, and pickled chiles.

Also beware of the goodies that tempt you at the salad bar. Grated cheese, bacon bits, fried croutons, olives, avocados, and sour cream can also skyrocket the fat grams contained in what once might have been an innocent salad. Use the goodies in moderation or not at all.

USE FLAVORFUL LETTUCES SUCH AS FIELD GREENS AND ROMAINE. USE ICEBERG FOR THE CRUNCH.

Lettuce is mostly water. If you use a bland lettuce like iceberg you will be tempted to add flavor with more dressing!

AFTER WASHING YOUR GREENS, DRY THEM COMPLETELY. Dressing slides off wet greens. You will then tend to add more dressing to a bowl of slippery greens.

My friend Michael Harryman is a consummate lettuce drier and jazz tuba player (perhaps the two crafts are interrelated); he approaches lettuce drying like an art. His salads are like bouquets of greenery floating in the salad bowl. Dry your washed lettuces with paper towels, blotting all the little crevices or spin in a lettuce drier. Wrap lettuce in paper towels and place in plastic bag. Store in refrigerator for up to 3 days.

ADD COLORFUL TIDBITS FOR CRUNCH AND COLOR. Try cooked beans like garbanzos or black beans; cooked small pastas; raw and briefly steamed vegetables; reduced-fat cheese or Asiago cheese used in small amounts over top of salad where your eyes can enjoy it; homemade baked croutons are good also.

TURKEY CHIPOTLE TOSTADA

This is a good recipe to make with leftover turkey or broiled turkey tenderloins. Marinate tenderloins in a little olive oil, lemon juice, garlic, and cilantro and grill or broil.

PER SERVING:
307 calories
34 g protein
24 g carbohydrate
7 g fat
74 mg cholesterol
368 mg sodium

2 turkey tenderloins, about 12 ounces each
2 teaspoons olive oil
3 tablespoons lime or lemon juice
Chipotle Dressing: Makes 3/4 cup
1/4 cup reduced-fat mayonnaise
1/2 cup nonfat yogurt
Juice from 1 lime
1 clove garlic, minced through press
1 canned chipotle chile
1 teaspoon adobo sauce from can
6 flour tortillas (7-inches)
6 cups romaine lettuce, dried and torn
1/2 cup thinly sliced red onion
8 cherry tomatoes, washed and halved
1/4 cup grated reduced-fat Monterey Jack cheese
1/4 cup cilantro, snipped with scissors

Rub tenderloins with olive oil and lime juice. Broil or grill or about 10 minutes per side. Slice for the tostada salad.

For Chipotle Dressing, combine mayonnaise, yogurt, lime juice, garlic, chipotle, adobo sauce, and cilantro.

Place tortillas on a baking sheet and bake in preheated 375 degree oven for about 8 minutes or until tortillas are crisp around the edges. Watch carefully.

Place crisped tortillas on plates. Heap 1 cup romaine on each one, add onion slices, sliced turkey, and cherry tomatoes. Drizzle over the tops of the tostada salads with 2 tablespoons of Chipotle Dressing. Sprinkle tops with grated cheese and cilantro.

6 servings.

Note: you can add Pickled Pink Onions to the salads in place of just sliced, raw onion. In Mexico, the pickled onions are added to salads, torta sandwiches, and as a topping for enchiladas.

PICKLED PINK ONIONS

These give a flavor boost to the simplest offering. I keep them in a pickle jar in the refrigerator so they are always available to add to quick tacos, tostada salads, and tortas.

1 cup apple cider vinegar
1/2 cup rice vinegar
1/2 cup water
1 tablespoon olive oil
2 teaspoons oregano
1 bay leaf
5 crushed peppercorns
2 sliced medium red onions

Simmer vinegars, water, olive oil, oregano, bay leaf, and peppercorns in a saucepan just for 2 minutes. Immediately pour over the red onions in a heatproof bowl. Steep for at least 1 hour before using. They will turn a

PER SERVING:
34 calories
.51 g protein
5 g carbohydrate
2 g fat
0 mg cholesterol
1 mg sodium

pretty pink color which is the main reason for using the red onions. Stored in a jar in the refrigerator they will keep well for a month.

Makes 1 pint. Serves 6.

CHICKEN TOSTADA
WITH GRAPE SALSA

PER SERVING:
288 calories
26 g protein
21 g carbohydrate
10 g fat
67 mg cholesterol
199 mg sodium

Trust me on this one. Grape Salsa is one of those palate surprises that you may not believe until you try it. All of my official tasters can't get enough of it.

2 cups seedless flame, purple, or Thompson grapes, sliced in half
1 tablespoon lemon juice
1 tablespoon rice vinegar
1 teaspoon olive oil
1 clove garlic, minced through press
1 fresh jalapeño chile, seeded, finely minced
2 tablespoon chives, snipped
2 tablespoons cilantro, snipped with scissors
4 tablespoons toasted almond slivers, crushed
1/8 teaspoon salt
1/8 teaspoon cayenne pepper
1/4 teaspoon freshly ground pepper
6 small flour tortillas
Canola oil spray
1/2 cup light sour cream (40% less fat)
1 tablespoon frozen apple juice concentrate, thawed
3 cups dried romaine lettuce, chopped
3 cups cooked chicken breast, cut into strips

For the grape salsa, stir together the halved grapes, lemon juice, rice vinegar, olive oil, garlic, jalapeño, chives, cilantro, toasted almonds, salt, cayenne pepper, and freshly ground pepper. Makes 2 and 1/4 cups.

Brush the tortillas lightly with oil and bake in a pre-heated 375 degree oven until they are crisp, about 8 minutes. Watch carefully.

Stir together the sour cream and frozen apple juice for dressing.

Place the crisp tortillas on 6 plates and cover with shredded lettuce, chicken, about 1/3 cup Grape Salsa for each tostada. Drizzle a tablespoon of the light sour cream dressing over the top.

Serves 6 as a light lunch.

THE BEST CHICKEN TOSTADA SALAD WITH CREAMY MEX DRESSING

The Parkway Grill in Pasadena makes a state-of-the-art chicken tostada which serves as my supreme model. You and I, as home cooks, will only diverge from their example by not smoking our chicken in a brick oven but our dressing will taste just as good even though we're cutting back on the virgin olive oil.

Creamy Mex Dressing:
1 clove garlic
1 shallot
1 green onion or 1 tablespoon fresh chives

PER SERVING:
621 calories
48 g protein
59 g carbohydrate
21 g fat
95 mg cholesterol
1012 mg sodium

1 tablespoon grainy Dijon mustard
1/2 teaspoon salt
1 teaspoon red chile powder
1 tablespoon cilantro
1 tablespoon balsamic vinegar
1 tablespoon lime juice or lemon juice
1 tablespoon rice vinegar
1 tablespoon olive oil
4 tablespoons orange juice
1/2 cup reduced-fat sour cream
6 boned, skinned chicken breast filets
Juice of 2 limes
1 and 1/2 cups cooked black beans (recipe below)
  or use drained canned black beans
2 ears fresh corn (if in season), kernels cut off cobs or
  sub with canned niblets, 1 and 1/4 cups
1 and 1/2 quarts combination of romaine and red leaf
  lettuce, washed and dried, torn into small pieces
1 and 1/2 cups grated reduced-fat Monterey Jack
  cheese
1 avocado, sliced
12 cherry tomatoes, halved
6 10-inch flour tortillas

Note: believe it or not this is a healthy version of a tostada salad using a dressing with less oil, reduced-fat cheese, reduced-fat sour cream, and less avocado. It's still high in calories, fat, and sodium. Imagine what a full-fat tostada salad chalks up!!

First make the Creamy Mex Dressing so it can be chilling and thickening in the refrigerator. Into bowl of food processor or blender jar, place garlic, shallot, green onion, mustard, salt, chile powder, cilantro, balsamic vinegar, lime juice, rice vinegar, olive oil, orange juice, and sour cream. Blend until of smooth consistency. Refrigerate until needed.

Squeeze lime juice over chicken and broil or grill (on oiled grill) for about 8 minutes per side. Set aside to cool and then cut into strips.

Drain the cooked black beans. If they are cold from the refrigerator, warm them in microwave or in a saucepan.

Steam the corn kernels. Crisp the tortillas into attractive tostada shells; spray both sides of each tortilla with olive oil or canola oil mist. Drape a tortilla upside down over a microwave-safe 3-cup mixing bowl. Microwave tortilla on high power for about 160 seconds. Turn every 60 seconds. The tortilla shell will harden into a crisp tostada bowl. Repeat with the remaining flour tortillas.

The Presentation: Place the crisp tostada shells on plates and divide up the lettuce, broiled chicken strips, black beans and corn. Drizzle 2 tablespoons Creamy Mex Dressing over each tostada. Garnish with grated cheese, avocado, and cherry tomatoes. Pass more dressing at the table for the indulgent. Serves 6.

BLACK BEANS FOR SALADS AND TOSTADAS

For a salad you want the beans to be firm and appetizingly black so they do not require a presoaking or long cooking time. If you need beans in large amounts, just double the recipe. Black beans can also be pressure cooked in 30 minutes. The beans freeze quite well.

1 cup or 1/2 pound black beans
4 cups water
1/2 cup chopped onion
2 cloves garlic
1/2 teaspoon salt

PER SERVING:
135 calories
8 g protein
25 g carbohydrate
.56 g fat
0 mg cholesterol
185 mg sodium

Rinse beans off in cold, running water and search for stones. Place in a 2-quart pot and cover with 4 cups water and rest of ingredients except the salt. Adding the salt too early can cause the beans to remain hard. Simmer on low for about 1 and 1/2 hours. Add the salt during the last 15 minutes. Check on the beans and taste them as you want them to be cooked and yet firm.

6 servings

TACO SALAD WITH SALSA DRESSING

I have tried to do non-fat taco salads but that good, old-fashioned taste is missing. This version is lower in fat: not so low it scares you away but good enough for you to make it again and again. The Salsa Dressing gives it life.

Salsa Dressing:
3 tablespoons balsamic vinegar
3 tablespoons lemon juice
1/4 cup water
2 tablespoons olive oil
1 teaspoon Dijon mustard
1 clove garlic, minced through a press
1 tomato, juiced and seeded
1 pickled jalapeño chile
1/4 cup cilantro
1/4 teaspoon salt
Taco Meat for Salad:
8 ounces ground sirloin
8 ounces ground turkey breast
2 teaspoons dried oregano
2 teaspoons ground red chile powder
1/2 teaspoon ground cumin

PER SERVING:
291 calories
24 g protein
17 g carbohydrate
12 g fat
63 mg cholesterol
520 mg sodium

1/2 teaspoon salt
3 cups dried romaine, torn into pieces
1 cup grated reduced-fat Cheddar
2 cups fat-free baked corn chips

   Using a food processor, blend vinegar, lemon juice, water, olive oil, mustard and garlic until thickened. Then add pieces of tomato, chile, cilantro, and salt. Blend until just tiny bits of chile and cilantro show. I use this dressing frequently with tossed salads and vegetables. Makes 1 and 1/4 cup dressing.

   Spray a nonstick 10-inch skillet with olive oil or canola oil mist. Fry the ground sirloin and turkey, breaking it up with a spatula. As it cooks sprinkle with the oregano, chile powder, cumin, and salt.

   On a large platter, toss the lettuce with 1/2 cup of the Salsa Dressing or some of the Guacamole Dressing (recipe given below) Then add the cooked meat, grated cheese, and the tortilla chips. If you like, garnish the salad with tomato slices and slices of Jalapeño Carrots.

   Serves 6.

JALAPEÑO CARROTS

PER SERVING:
69 calories
1 g protein
11 g carbohydrate
3 g fat
0 mg cholesterol
171 mg sodium

I am mad about these Mexican carrots and put them in tuna salad sandwiches, taco salads, dips, and serve them for noshing. This recipe calls for less olive oil than the original.

2 bunches of carrots (about 2 pounds), peeled
1 and 1/2 cups apple cider vinegar
3/4 cup water
2 tablespoons olive oil
2 to 3 bay leaves
1 onion, sliced thinly
5-8 canned jalapeño chiles, some seeds removed

Cut carrots into 3-inch diagonal pieces and place in steamer basket over simmering water. Steam for 5 minutes so carrots remain crisp.

While the carrots are steaming, combine the vinegar, water, olive oil, bay leaves, sliced onion, and jalapeños ingredients in a large bowl. Dump the hot carrots into the bowl . Stir from time to time. The various flavors will penetrate after a couple of hours of steeping. Store in a glass jar. Serve on a bed of parsley or cilantro accompanied by sticks of sharp cheese or use them in everything. 10 servings.

GUACAMOLE DRESSING

PER SERVING:
Per Tablespoon
21 calories
.55 g protein
1 g carbohydrate
1 g fat
0 mg cholesterol
21 mg sodium

This delicious dressing gives you an alternative or use a little of this and a little of the Salsa Dressing, page 46.

1 ripe avocado
1 tablespoon lemon juice
1 teaspoon hot pepper sauce
1 clove minced garlic
3 minced green onions
1/2 cup nonfat yogurt
2 tablespoons green salsa, homemade or bottled

In bowl, mash the avocado with lemon juice, pepper sauce, garlic, green onions, nonfat yogurt, and green salsa. Makes about 1 and 1/4 cups or 6 servings.

THE CAPTAIN'S CAESAR SALAD

PER SERVING:
219 calories
7 g protein
11 g carbohydrate
17 g fat
6 mg cholesterol
407 mg sodium

This salad enjoys a Mexican birthright, having been created by Caesar Cardini in Tiajuana and now recreated the world over. The calories of the classic preparation have been reduced but it is not a low-fat salad. Enjoy it as we do on special occasions.

One of the best Caesar Salads I ever ate was on a 62-foot ketch anchored off one of the British Virgin Islands. The captain was in a testy mood because the dinghy had a new leak. He told us that we couldn't sail on to the next island.

Molly, the cook poked her head out of the hatch to inform him she was not spending the night because it was much better to go on to Cooper's Island, a better anchorage. In between mouthfuls of Caesar Salad the captain told the cook that he knew where to go and when. The cook told the captain that she knew where he should go. She didn't mean Cooper's Island. We leaned back, sipping the icy margarita that Molly had handed us when we came dripping out of the salty water. The captain told Molly he would take away her passport and throw her off the boat for insubordination. We all protested. No one could make a Caesar Salad like Molly.

We took the captain aside and asked him a question we all knew the answer to, "Can you cook?" He looked at the leaky dinghy, which was less than Captain Bly himself had. We went on to Cooper's Island where Molly served Lobster Curry for dinner and we all wore fresh T-shirts and toasted the captain for knowing a good cook never gives up the ship.

2 heads of romaine lettuce
2 cloves garlic, minced through press
2 teaspoons anchovy paste
2 teaspoons Dijon mustard
1 and 1/2 teaspoons Worcestershire sauce
1/4 teaspoon freshly ground black pepper
2 tablespoons lemon juice (1 lemon)
1/3 cup good flavorful olive oil
2 tablespoons + 1/4 cup Parmesan cheese

1 and 1/2 cups cubed French bread for croutons
1 clove garlic, minced with a press
1 tablespoon olive oil

Wash the lettuce, pulling off the outer leaves and reserving for another salad. Use the hearts of each romaine for this salad as it is most delicious if you eat with your fingers. Dry leaves with paper towels.

Blend garlic, anchovy paste, mustard, Worcestershire sauce, pepper, lemon juice, olive oil, and 2 tablespoons of Parmesan. This will help thicken the dressing so that it clings to the lettuce.

Place bread cubes on a cookie sheet. Combine the minced clove of garlic and 1 tablespoon of olive oil. Brush on croutons. Bake in a preheated 375 degree oven until golden, about 10 minutes. Watch carefully. Stir the croutons once so they bake evenly.

Drizzle part of dressing over the greens, placed in a large, wide salad bowl. Lift up the greens gently, adding more dressing and the croutons. Sprinkle liberally with the grated cheese and serve.

Serves 6.

WARM SPAGHETTI SALAD WITH SALSA

PER SERVING:
381 calories
14 g protein
62 g carbohydrate
9 g fat
62 mg cholesterol
169 mg sodium

When I want something beautiful, easy and good, this is what I serve. The contrast of the warm pasta with the salsa is one of the best. This spaghetti was frantically invented while we still lived in Querétaro, Mexico

One leisurely afternoon, there was a loud knock on the door and my maid, Pueblito came to tell me that there were six elegantes (well-dressed people) standing outside. My husband, the director of a private school, had invited visiting student teachers from Pennsylvania to an early dinner and forgotten to tell me. They thanked me for the invitation as they had heard reports that I was a gourmet cook.

I thought of various way to murder my husband. After tucking them into the sala, I sprinted for the kitchen and sent Pueblito running out the back door chanting Madre de Dios to see if the neighbors had any spaghetti. Pueblito, usually not known for speed, was back in minutes with two packages of spaghetti

I found 5 ripe tomatoes, garlic, chiles, a wedge of Parmesan cheese, and one can of smoked sturgeon. Hurriedly, we made a salsa fresca and boiled spaghetti. My husband came in the door looking sheepish but having too many witnesses, I couldn't do anything to him YET. With great flourish, the spaghetti was tossed at the table with olive oil, salsa, grated Parmesan cheese and several grinds of fresh pepper. The guests thought it was an old Mexican recipe and my husband has never repeated his folly.

4 ripe tomatoes, diced with skins on
1 clove garlic, minced through press
1 jalapeño chile, seeded and minced
1/2 cup red onion, diced
1/2 cup red or green bell pepper
1 tablespoons red wine vinegar
1 teaspoon olive oil
Freshly ground pepper and salt to taste
2 tablespoons cilantro, snipped with scissors, optional
1 pound dried spaghetti
2 tablespoon olive oil
1 clove garlic, minced through a press
1 teaspoon Tabasco
1/2 cup grated Parmesan Reggiano cheese
Freshly ground black pepper to taste
Red pepper flakes to taste

Combine diced tomatoes, garlic, jalapeño, red onion, red pepper, vinegar, olive oil, salt, pepper, and cilantro. Set aside the salsa fresca.

Combine the olive oil, garlic, and Tabasco.

Bring a pot of water to a boil and add the spaghetti. Cook until it is al dente, about 8 to 10 minutes. Drain. Do not rinse. To serve immediately place the hot spaghetti on a platter and toss with the warm olive oil-garlic mixture. Then toss with the salsa fresca, the grated Parmesan, and some freshly grated black pepper. Pass more grated cheese and red pepper flakes at the table. Serves 4 to 6 people depending upon whether or not you are offering salad and bread (or a can of sturgeon).

6 servings

JICAMA AND RED PEPPER SALAD

PER SERVING:
97 calories
2 g protein
13 g carbohydrate
5 g fat
0 mg cholesterol
43 mg sodium

Originally I came up with this recipe for *The Salsa Book.* It is an example of how easily a chopped salsa can become a salad and I could not resist including it in this chapter. Its crunchiness is a perfect complement to Southwestern foods and I would choose it any day over the more traditional Christmas salad of jicama, oranges, and beets. It's also a great diet salad if you cut the oil down to the barest minimum of a couple of teaspoons.

1 small jicama (1 pound), peeled
3 carrots, peeled
1 red bell pepper
1 small red onion, peeled
1 to 2 jalapeño chiles, seeded
2 cloves garlic, minced through a press
1/2 cup rice vinegar
2 tablespoons canola oil or olive oil
1/4 teaspoon freshly ground black pepper
1/2 teaspoon crushed red pepper flakes
2 teaspoons dried oregano
Pinch of salt
3 to 4 tablespoons cilantro, snipped with scissors

Dice the vegetables into equal sizes. Whisk together the garlic, rice vinegar, oil, black and red pepper, oregano, salt, and cilantro. Pour the dressing over the vegetables and marinate for at least 2 hours before serving. Use the minimum amount of oil if you are watching your intake of fats.

Serves 6 as an accompaniment or side dish.

BASQUE SALAD

In Arizona, Nevada, and, California there are small communities with Basque hotels serving families, sheepherders, and trenchermen who know about the good food. It is my style of food because they use a lot of garlic. This refreshing salad is similar to the Greek style salad, the only difference being that the Basque cooks use goat cheese instead of feta. With a hunk of rough bread, I have often made a meal out of just this salad.

2 ripe tomatoes, diced (2 cups)
1 cucumber, peeled, diced (1 cup)
1 red onion, peeled and chopped (1 cup)
1 red or green bell pepper, diced (1 cup)
1 clove garlic, minced through a press
2 tablespoons red wine vinegar
2 teaspoons dried oregano
Pinch of salt
1/2 teaspoon black pepper
2 tablespoons flavorful olive oil
1/2 cup crumbled mild goat cheese or feta cheese
   (4 ounces)

Combine all the diced vegetables with the dressing ingredients and the crumbled cheese. It is best if it marinates together for at least 1 hour.

6 servings

PER SERVING:
85 calories
3 g protein
6 g carbohydrate
6 g fat
9 mg cholesterol
86 mg sodium

PEAR SALAD

In wintertime when I want a refreshing change I often turn to this salad. Everyone seems to love the combination and I never make enough.

PER SERVING:
206 calories
5 g protein
17 g carbohydrate
14 g fat
8 mg cholesterol
168 mg sodium

1 head of red leaf lettuce, washed and dried
1 cup spinach leaves, washed and dried
3 pears
1/2 cup roughly chopped walnuts, toasted
1/2 cup crumbled blue cheese or Roquefort cheese
1/3 cup raspberry vinegar
1/2 teaspoon dry mustard
1/2 teaspoon freshly ground pepper
1/2 teaspoon sugar
2 tablespoons sunflower oil

Toast the walnuts for only 8 minutes in a 350 degree oven until they are only very lightly toasted. Set aside.

Mix up the raspberry vinegar, dry mustard, pepper, sugar, and oil.

Just before serving time, tear up the lettuce and spinach and place in a bowl. Peel the pears, core, and cut into paper-thin slices. Crumble in the blue cheese and walnuts. Toss the salad with the dressing, adding the pear slices. Reserve a few slices for garnish.

Serves 6.

GRAPEFRUIT, ORANGE, AND AVOCADO SALAD WITH TEXAS DRESSING

For many years, the legendary Helen Corbitt directed the restaurants for Neiman-Marcus and the Greenhouse in Dallas; she was amused that a simple poppy seed dressing caused such a big stir. Even those big Texas men loved the dressing so much, Helen caught them putting it on their potatoes.

PER SERVING:
230 calories
2 g protein
18 g carbohydrate
18 g fat
0 mg cholesterol
54 mg sodium

1/4 cup chopped onion (preferably red)
1 teaspoon dry mustard
1/4 teaspoon salt
1/2 teaspoon celery seeds
1 and 1/2 tablespoons poppy seeds
1/4 cup brown sugar
1/3 cup cider vinegar (do not use wine vinegar)
2 tablespoons lemon juice (1 lemon)
2/3 cup mild oil
2 tablespoons honey
1 head of red leaf lettuce, washed and dried
2 oranges
1 grapefruit
1 ripe but firm avocado
6 large ripe but firm strawberries (optional)

Note: 2 tablespons of poppyseed dressing is 133 calories with 13 g. fat. Use just 1 and 1/2 tablespoons on your own tossed salad if you want to "go below" 10 g. fat.

In the bowl of a food processor, place onion, dry mustard, salt, celery seeds, poppy seeds, brown sugar, vinegar, lemon juice and sunflower oil. Puree to a smooth consistency. I have tried adding only 1/2 cup of oil but the dressing is very thin in this case. By adding 2/3 cup oil, the dressing is thick and emulsified. Refrigerate dressing in a glass jar. It will thicken with chilling.

Cut off the tops and bottoms of oranges and grapefruit

with a sharp knife and then peel from top to bottom, cutting away the white membranes completely. Slice the oranges. Cut the grapefruit slices into smaller quarters. Slice the avocado right before serving time so it does not turn brownish.

The dressing is higher in sugar and oil than any other dressing in this chapter but small amounts are sufficient for flavor. Arrange the torn lettuce in a large shallow dish and toss with half of the fruit and a couple of tablespoons of dressing. Arrange the rest of the fruit slices and avocado slices artistically around the salad and drizzle more dressing on top. Use 1/3 cup dressing total when tossing the salad and pass more at the table (in case someone wants to put it on his potatoes).

Makes 1 and 1/2 cups or 6 servings.

RED CABBAGE AND APPLE SALAD
WITH POPPY SEED DRESSING

PER SERVING:
148 calories
1 g protein
22 g carbohydrate
7 g fat
0 mg cholesterol
21 mg sodium

Here is another healthy way to use the poppy seed dressing.

3 cups thinly sliced and chopped red cabbage
2 Golden Delicious apples, peeled, cored, chopped
1/2 cup raisins
1/4 cup pecans, toasted and roughly chopped
3 tablespoons poppy seed dressing (recipe above)

Pour a couple of tablespoons of boiling water over the

raisins to plump or place in a small glass dish and microwave the raisins on high power for 50 seconds.

After slicing and chopping the cabbage and apples, toss with all of the ingredients. Kids love this salad when it is slathered with lots of the poppy seed dressing. You can always keep their half of the salad in a separate bowl with more dressing.

Serves 6 as a small separate salad or side dish.

MEXICAN COLE SLAW

This recipe was inspired by a salad created by Texas chef, Dean Fearing. It is a perfect accompaniment to barbecues; I sometimes serve it with salpicòn.

3 cups finely shredded cabbage
1 cup shredded, peeled carrots
1/2 cup diced red bell pepper
1/2 cup minced cilantro
Dressing:
1/2 cup reduced-fat mayonnaise
2 tablespoons maple syrup
1/2 tablespoon Dijon mustard
1 tablespoon rice vinegar
1 tablespoon lime juice
1/4 teaspoon ground cumin
1/4 teaspoon salt
1 jalapeño chile, stemmed, seeded and minced

PER SERVING:
93 calories
0 g protein
13 g carbohydrate
4 g fat
0 mg cholesterol
302 mg sodium

For dressing mix together the mayonnaise, maple syrup, mustard, rice vinegar, lime juice, cumin, salt, and jalapeño chile.

Combine the cabbage, carrots, bell pepper, and cilantro in a large bowl. Add two-thirds of the dressing. Toss to combine. (If you like a creamier slaw, add all of the dressing.) Refrigerate for at least 2 hours before serving. Stores well up to 1 day in refrigerator.

Serves 6.

NEW MEXICAN POTATO SALAD

PER SERVING:
259 calories
5 g protein
40 g carbohydrate
10 g fat
0 mg cholesterol
496 mg sodium

The charm to this salad is that it is much lower in fat than the usual mayonnaise-laden potato salad but high on spices and flavor, naturally attracting avid devotees.

The spicy dressing is best when you use New Mexican red chile powder.

Note: cut fat and sodium more by reducing amount of black olives to 1/4 cup.

2 pounds red-skinned potatoes, well-scrubbed
2 tablespoons wine vinegar
1 cup diced red bell pepper
1/2 cup diced green bell pepper
1 bunch green onions, chopped
1 can Mexicorn, 11 ounces
1/2 cup sliced black olives
1 tablespoon cilantro, snipped
New Mexican Dressing:
1 clove garlic, minced
1 teaspoon Dijon mustard
1/2 teaspoon salt

2 teaspoons ground red New Mexican chile
1/4 teaspoon ground cumin
2 tablespoons wine vinegar
3 tablespoons olive oil
Freshly ground black pepper

Steam the potatoes for 30 minutes or until tender when pierced with a knife. While the potatoes are cooking, prepare the vegetables and dressing.

For the spicy dressing, combine garlic, mustard, salt, red chile, cumin, wine vinegar, and olive oil.

When potatoes are cooked, drain in a colander and cool for 5 minutes. Place the warm potatoes on a chopping board. Slice them and cut them into cubes. Put cubed potatoes into a bowl and douse with 2 tablespoons wine vinegar. Gently stir. Next add the dressing, peppers, green onions, corn kernels, olives and cilantro. Grind fresh pepper over the salad which is marvelous for picnics and barbecues.

Serves 6.

RED PEPPER CILANTRO PESTO TORTE

This colorful torte, with its layers of red and green, is a work of art. Serve it as an appetizer with raw vegetables like jicama and cucumbers. Also delicious with crackers or slices of baguette.

PER SERVING:
148 calories
7 g protein
6 g carbohydrate
11 g fat
23 mg cholesterol
209 mg sodium

1 teaspoon olive oil
1/4 cup shallots
2 cups part-skim ricotta cheese (1 pound)
8 ounces reduced-fat cream cheese
2 cloves garlic, minced through a press
6 ounces peeled red peppers from jar
2 teaspoons red chile powder
1/2 teaspoon ground cumin
2 tablespoons canned jalapeño chiles, minced
Cilantro Pesto:
2 cups cilantro leaves
1/4 cup grated Asiago cheese
2 tablespoons toasted pumpkin seeds (pepitas)
2 cloves garlic
1 tablespoon lime juice
3 tablespoons olive oil
12-inch by 12-inch double thickness cheesecloth
1-quart mold or strainer
Sliced black olives and cilantro leaves for garnish

Heat olive oil and sauté the shallots until soft but not brown, for about 3 minutes.

Using a food processor beat the ricotta cheese and cream cheese until smooth. Blend in the sauteed shallots, garlic, the red peppers, red chile, cumin, and jalapeño chiles. Puree until smooth.

Remove the cheese mixture from the processor and set aside. Wipe out and add cilantro, Asiago, pumpkin seeds, garlic, lime juice, and olive oil. Blend into a smooth pesto.

Rinse the piece of cheesecloth in cold water and wring out. Use it to line a 6-cup mold. I use one of the white porcelain molds which has holes for drainage. You could even use a small clean terra-cotta flower pot. Or just line a wire strainer with the cheesecloth. Use half of the red cheese mixture as the first layer. Place the pesto layer next. Finish with the rest of the cheese mixture as the last layer. Fold the ends of the cheesecloth over the top and press into the red cheese mixture. Stand your mold over a plate (my mold has little feet) or if using strainer, place over a bowl to catch the drips of whey from the ricotta cheese. Cover with plastic wrap and refrigerate for several hours or overnight.

To unmold, fold back the cheesecloth. Place a serving dish on top and turn over. Tap on counter. Gently lift off mold and peel off the cheesecloth which will leave a pretty texture on the torte. Garnish with chopped cilantro and olives.

Serves 12 guests

MARINATED JICAMA STICKS

Jicama is the Mexican root vegetable with a skin resembling that of a Russet potato. Peel off the brownish skin with a sharp paring knife to reveal the snowy white interior with a crisp texture. Street vendors in Mexico sell slices of jicama, offering you wedges of lime and packets of chile powder for seasoning. I like to marinate jicama sticks in lemon juice and cilantro for snacking.

PER SERVING:
13 calories
0 g protein
3 g carbohydrate
0 g fat
0 mg cholesterol
50 mg sodium

These are also good with the torte.

4 slices of peeled jicama
1/4 cup lemon juice
1/4 cup cold water
1/4 teaspoon salt
1/4 cup minced cilantro
1/2 teaspoon red chile powder for sprinkling

Cut jicama into sticks and place in bowl. Combine lemon juice, water, salt, and cilantro; pour over the jicama and marinate for at least 1 hour. Just before serving, remove the jicama from marinade and place on small serving dish. Sprinkle with red chile.

Serves 4 to 6.

SKINNY GUACAMOLE

PER SERVING:
1   tablespoon
14 calories
0 g protein
1 g carbohydrate
1 g fat
0 mg cholesterol
77 mg sodium

I know you want the real stuff. But it's loaded with fat especially if you just can't stop dipping and dipping into it. You will be surprised at how much you will like Skinny Guacamole. I even spread it on my torta sandwiches instead of mayonnaise.

1/2 cup mashed avocado
1/2 cup plain nonfat yogurt
1 tablespoon lemon juice
2 cloves of minced garlic
1 teaspoon garlic salt
1 tablespoon grated onion
2 serrano chiles, finely minced with the seeds

1/4 cup minced tomato
1/4 cup minced cilantro

Combine avocado, yogurt, lemon juice, garlic, garlic salt, onion (grate on big holes of cheese grater), chiles, tomato, and cilantro. Use a fork to mash everything together, working toward a coarse texture which is part of the charm of real classic Mexican guacamole.

Serve with the new nonfat baked tortilla chips, slices of cucumber, red bell pepper, and yes, more of the jicama sticks. For a party, I cut off the tops of red bell peppers and remove the seeds. Use pepper shells as containers for "guac."

Serves 6

Note: stir a couple of teaspoons of pureed chipotle en adobo into the guacamole for even more spicy heat.

BLACK BEAN DIP

This velvety concoction is not only good for dipping but it can raise your Mexican noshing to new levels. Spread inside soft tacos before filling with grilled chicken and salsa. Smear it onto halved French rolls or bolillos from the panadería; lay thin slices of reduced-fat Jack cheese on top of the beans and broil until bubbly. You will most likely even think of more things to do with Black Bean Dip.

1 19-ounce can drained black beans
  or use 1 and 1/2 cups homemade beans
2 cloves minced garlic
2 jalapeño chiles, seeded and minced

PER SERVING:
106 calories
6 g protein
15 g carbohydrate
3 g fat
7 mg cholesterol
304 mg sodium

1 tablespoon lime juice
1 tablespoon apple cider vinegar
1/4 teaspoon ground cumin
2 teaspoons ground red chile powder
1 3-ounce package reduced-fat cream cheese

In bowl of food processor, place black beans, garlic, chiles, lime juice, vinegar, cumin, red chile, and cream cheese. Blend until smooth.

Spray a shallow, heatproof baking dish (3-cup size) with olive oil or canola oil mist. Fill with the Black Bean Dip. Bake in preheated 375 degree oven for 15 minutes.

Serves 6 as appetizer. Recipe doubles easily for more people. Analysis based on homemade black beans.

TORTILLA TURKEY ROLL-UPS

When brought to a party, they never fail to bring on the recipe requests. No one wants to know how to do the complicated, classic dishes that take hours in the kitchen.

PER SERVING:
195 calories
15 g protein
14 g carbohydrate
9 g fat
44 mg cholesterol
569 mg sodium

11 ounces reduced-fat cream cheese, softened
2 teaspoons grainy mustard
1 to 2 minced pickled jalapeño chiles
1 tablespoon jalapeño juice from can
1 tablespoon ground red chile powder
   or 1/4 teaspoon cayenne powder
3 minced green onions
1/4 cup sliced black olives

2 tablespoons minced jalapeño carrots (optional)
2 tablespoons minced cilantro
6 very fresh low-fat flour tortillas (60% less fat)
2 cups slivered red leaf or other colorful lettuce
1/2 pound paper thin slices turkey breast

Note: if you have any pureed chipotle en adobo such as Don Alfonso's, add 2 teaspoons to the cream cheese mixture.

Place cream cheese in a bowl. Use wooden spoon to blend in mustard, chiles, jalapeño juice, red chile, green onions, black olives, carrots, and cilantro. Taste to see if you want to add more of something, like more chile powder!

Spread equal amounts of the cream cheese mixture over each flour tortilla. Top with a little lettuce and gently press into the cheese. Arrange 3 slices overlapping slices of turkey over the lettuce. Tightly roll up each tortilla and roll up in plastic wrap to seal. Refrigerate at least 2 hours before serving so that flavors may blend and moisture penetrates the tortillas.

Slice each roll into 6 pinwheels. Find someone to eat the ragged edges. Arrange roll-ups on a bed of lettuce or watercress.

Serves 8 as appetizer.

SOPAS

CHAPTER III

THE SOUPS OF MEXICO

he soul of Mexican cuisine is the soup, drawing greatly on the country's Spanish heritage. Mexico even experienced a period of romantic inclination toward anything French, particularly during the rule of Porfirio Díaz. I have eaten creamed soups in small family restaurants which were French in their delicacy but they were made with Indian squash or the truffle-like huitlacoche.

Mexicans will make soup out of almost anything—roots, peelings, chicken feet, marrow bones, stomach lining (tripe), tomato skins, and wild herbs. Latin cuisine excels in utilizing everything from skin to bones.

Homemade caldo, or broth, provides the essence for all soups. Unlike American cooks, Mexican cooks take a relaxed attitude toward making caldo. If you simmer your soup base for a long time, you can tenderize tough cuts of meat into succulent bites and you do not have to use a great deal of meat. My Spanish-Californian grandmother used meats for seasoning rather than a main ingredient.

When you cook vegetables in the caldo, their essence and nourishment goes into the broth rather than escaping into steam. Soup is a wonderful medium for the jewels of unusual grains—barley, basmati rice, colorful beans, or cracked wheat. Many people who won't eat brown rice will happily eat it in soup.

For me, soup is one of the most soul-satisfying parts of a meal. If you have a bowl of soup as a first course, you will have a sensation of being full, indulging in less of the rest of the meal. In fact, I'm contented to make my entire meal a good bowl of soup.

DO NOT BE AFRAID OF STOCKS

For beginning cooks, making stock can elicit the same fear as making bread or deglazing pans. It sounds fancy but isn't. If all you want to do is make stock out of a chicken and some water, do it.

Forget the 3-hour stock rule given by someone dressed in impeccable whites with a staff of fifteen. I never cook my chicken stock for 3 hours. Too much of a solid block of time to pay attention to the pot. I put a whole chicken, some water, and salt in my pressure cooker and simmer for about 50 minutes. I add celery, carrots, wine, salt, and herbs if I have them. Remember that the factory making canned broth isn't adding Chardonnay or leeks or fines herbs. Anything you do is better than the can. Or simply add some good ingredients to the canned stuff.

FEARLESS CHICKEN BROTH

Use this recipe when you want it quick. In 30 minutes you will have a base for soup.

1 quart fat-free reduced-sodium canned chicken broth
1 quart water
1/4 cup white wine
1/2 onion
2 smashed cloves garlic
1 tomato with skin, cut in half
1 stalk celery with leaves, chopped
1 carrot, scraped and chopped
Sprig of parsley and thyme
1 chicken breast, skinned (optional)

PER SERVING:
21 calories
2 g protein
2 g carbohydrate
0 g fat
0 mg cholesterol
328 mg sodium

In 3-quart pot place canned broth, water, wine, onion, garlic, tomato, celery and leaves, carrot, and herbs. Simmer for 25 minutes. Add chicken breast during last 20 minutes. Turn off heat and allow it to steep in broth for 10 minutes.

Remove chicken breast and set aside. Strain broth. Use broth as soup base and use the cooked chicken to add back to chicken soup or for salads or tostadas.

Makes about 2 quarts broth or 8 servings

FRIENDLY CHICKEN BROTH

PER SERVING:
43 calories
.6 g protein
6 g carbohydrate
2 g fat
0 mg cholesterol
4 mg sodium

1 whole chicken, 3 and 1/2 pounds, skin removed
1/2 onion
1 carrot, peeled and cut in chunks
6 cloves garlic (yes, that is correct)
1 stalk celery with leaves, cut into chunks
1 tomato, cut in half
1/2 cup of dry white wine
8 cups water
1 sprig parsley
1 sprig thyme or 1 teaspoon dried thyme
1 teaspoon salt (optional)
1/4 teaspoon pepper

Wash off the chicken in cold water, remove packet of inner parts and discard or reserve for another use. Remove skin and cut off any excess pieces of chicken fat. Place chicken, breast-side up, in a pressure cooker or large pot. I use my faithful 8-quart pressure cooker (with built-in safety valve) and I never make stock the long way any more. Pour liquid over the top of the chicken, leaving the breast above the liquid to steam, and add chopped vegetables, herbs and salt. I feel that you need some salt to bring out the flavors of chicken broth, but if you are on a salt-free diet, please omit. Make this broth even if you only have half of the vegetables. It will still be good.

Bring the pressure cooker to a simmer and cook on low for 50 minutes. If you are using a regular pot, simmer ingredients for 1 and 1/2 hours. The pressure cooker extracts all the flavor from the chicken and I think that the white wine helps draw nutrients from the chicken bones; old-fashioned cooks utilized vinegar for the same purpose. If you have a favorite herb like fresh oregano, dill, or sweet basil—use that in the broth. If you don't have any herbs, don't worry.

Allow your pressure cooker to cool down for at least 20 minutes. You can speed this up by placing the pot in the sink and running cold water over the lid. Once the pressure has dropped you will be able to safely remove the lid. New pressure cookers all have safety locks built in. Lift the chicken out and place on a dinner plate to cool. Strain the broth and chill so you can easily remove the fat on the surface.

Use the steamed chicken for returning to the broth for chicken soup (see Janet's Doorstep Chicken Soup) or use for salads. Immediately eat the 2 little nuggets of meat on sides of the chicken back and invoke the spirit of James Beard who loved these among many other simple pleasures.

Makes about 2 quarts chicken broth.

JANET BLANDINO REDMAN'S DOORSTEP CHICKEN SOUP

PER SERVING:
188 calories
14 g protein
21 g carbohydrate
5 g fat
31 mg cholesterol
375 mg sodium

Whenever I suffer a cold or a winter flu, I long for the healing soups of my mother and grandmother and their way of enveloping me in such bustling care that I almost wished to remain slightly under the weather.

Wrapped in a flannel blanket, while the smells of chicken soup wafted into the room, I usually waited impatiently for my tray. Ah, my memories of The Tray with the old Blue Willow bowl of chicken soup, soda crackers with a side dish of jelly, tiny pieces of cut up fruit, a delicate piece of sponge cake, and a new movie magazine. Perfect fodder for an invalid of my standing; that is, I am rarely a sick person without an appetite.

When I was sick last February and made the trip into town to buy my poor self something to cook into soup, I returned to find a dented aluminum pot, resembling Grandmama's old pot, sitting on my doorstep. It was sort of ghostly until I found the reproachful note from Janet scolding me for not being home in bed.

The pot was filled to the brim with the most chickeny chicken soup. This soup, a gift from heaven, is one of the best I have ever savored. According to Janet, her Nicaraguan grandmother always added the lemon juice and brown rice to make it as healthful as possible for invalids. This soup is so nourishing it will keep you from becoming an invalid. Power to garlic, chiles, and lemons!!!

2 quarts chicken broth (use either recipe above)
4 carrots, peeled and sliced
3/4 cup brown rice
6 cloves minced garlic
1/2 cup minced green onions
2 cups shredded chicken
1-2 fresh jalapeño chiles, seeded and minced
1/3 cup fresh lemon juice
1/2 to 2 teaspoons salt
1/4 cup cilantro, snipped with scissors

Bring broth to a simmer and add the carrots, brown rice, and garlic. Cook on low heat for 35 minutes.

During the last 5 minutes of cooking, add the green onions, shredded chicken, chiles, lemon juice, salt, and cilantro. Spoon into wide soup bowls and eat immediately so as to repair your soul and cure all of your ills. It has been medically proven that chicken soup cures colds but when it is given the Hispanic touch with jalapeño chiles, we have the double whammy effect.

Serves 8 or 1 sick person for about a week.

SOPA DE LIMA

PER SERVING:
232 calories
23 g protein
26 g carbohydrate
5 g fat
49 mg cholesterol
105 mg sodium

It just so happens that one of the most celebrated dishes of the Mexican state of Yucatan is a soup—sopa de lima or lime soup which is really just a chicken soup lavishly flavored with the region's limas agrias (sour limes). I make it with California limes, rather inauthentic but delicious. Because of the pungency of the limes and the roasted garlic flavor, this soup more than any of the others transports me back to San Miguel de Allende, Guanajuato. This soup is Mexico.

2 quarts of chicken broth, use either recipe at beginning of chapter
1 and 1/2 chicken breasts, skinned, about 24 ounces
1 teaspoon of oil
1 onion, chopped
1 and 1/2 cups green bell pepper, chopped
1 and 1/2 cups red bell pepper, chopped
1 mild Anaheim pepper, seeded and chopped (do not remove skin)
2 large tomatoes, roasted and finely chopped
4 cloves of garlic, minced
2 teaspoons oregano
1 bay leaf
1/3 cup fresh lime juice
6 corn tortillas, cut into thin strips
4 limes, cut into wedges
1/4 cup cilantro, snipped with scissors
2 jalapeño chiles, seeded and minced

Simmer the chicken breasts in the broth for 25 minutes, skimming off any foam on the surface. Then remove the cooked chicken and set aside while you prepare rest of soup.

In the teaspoon of oil, saute the onion, bell peppers, and the chopped Anaheim chile. Char the tomatoes over a flame or under a broiler to loosen the skins. Peel tomatoes and chop. Mince the garlic. Add onion mixture, tomatoes and garlic to the chicken broth.

Shred the chicken breast with your fingers and add to the broth along with oregano, bay leaf, and lime juice. Heat to a gentle simmer.

Spray both sides of the corn tortillas with canola oil mist. Squeeze lime juice over them. Cut into strips and bake in a preheated 350 degree oven for about 10 minutes or until crisp and golden. Reserve for garnishing soup.

Prepare little bowls of condiments: the lime wedges, the cilantro, the minced jalapeños, and tortilla strips. Ladle soup into bowls and sprinkle with the crisp tortilla strips. Each person can add condiments of their choice.

Serves 8.

MEXICAN MINESTRONE
WITH CILANTRO PESTO

PER SERVING:
367 calories
20 g protein
68 g carbohydrate
3 g fat
0 mg cholesterol
150 mg sodium

After the heat of Indian summer, I can barely wait each year for the first cold night of autumn, that first shock of darkness coming at five o'clock. Then I can make my *a la cinco de la tarde* soup which brings gladness to my kitchen.

With its profusion of beans, spinach pasta, and vegetables this soup will make you feel healthy. It has become a favorite in our family and for an informal gathering it is greatly appreciated along with bread and wine.

1 cup pinto beans
1 cup black beans
6 cups water
1 tablespoon olive oil
2 onions, chopped
2 red bell peppers, chopped
2 cloves garlic, minced
2 leeks, well-rinsed and chopped
2 quarts of chicken stock
2 cups crushed, canned tomatoes
1 sprig fresh rosemary or 1 teaspoon dried rosemary
1 teaspoon salt (optional)
1 to 2 teaspoons ground chile (like Dixon)
2 teaspoon oregano
3 zucchini, sliced
6 carrots, peeled and sliced
2 cups kale, chopped
1 cup cabbage, chopped
1 and 1/2 cups spinach or semolina macaroni

If you are in a hurry you could begin the recipe by substituting canned beans but it is best to drain them in a sieve and rinse away the salty residue under cold running water. Or to start from scratch, wash your dried beans under running water and remove any stones. Place them in a large pot and add water about 2 inches over the level of the beans. Bring to a boil, simmering briskly for 3 minutes. Turn off the heat and allow the beans to steep for at least 2 hours. Then pour off all of this simmering liquid and add 6 cups of fresh water. Bring to a boil and simmer until the beans are tender, about 1 hour and 30 minutes.

Meanwhile, sauté the onions, peppers, garlic, and leeks in the olive oil. You could reduce the amount of olive oil required to just 1 teaspoon if you are really watching fats. Just remember that when you are using a small amount of oil for sautéing, vegetables tend to stick and burn more easily. Use a nonstick pan and keep stirring.

After the beans are just tender, add the sautéed vegetable mixture, chicken stock, crushed tomatoes, rosemary, salt, ground chile, oregano, and the zucchini, carrots, kale, and cabbage. Simmer for 10 minutes and then stir in the macaroni. Simmer for another 10 minutes or until the macaroni is tender.

Serve in wide soup bowls and let each guest add a tablespoon of cilantro pesto. Some pesto addicts spread the pesto on bread instead of butter. The minestrone is also wonderful without the pesto.

Serves 8.

CILANTRO PESTO

PER SERVING:
31 calories
9 g protein
.4 g carbohydrate
3 g fat
2 mg cholesterol
38 mg sodium

This is one of those instances where the taste of the cilantro becomes milder rather than stronger. Rather than the 1/2 cup of oil required for traditional pesto, we are using 2 tablespoons. You can also use this pesto to toss with pasta or as spread on bread.

2 tablespoons olive oil
1/4 cup freshly grated Parmesan or Asiago cheese
2 cloves garlic
1 cup cilantro
1 teaspoon dried mild oregano
Juice from 1/2 lime

Place all of the above ingredients into the bowl of a food processor and blend into a rough texture. Store in refrigerator.

Makes 3/4 cup pesto or 12 servings, 1 T. each.

SOPA DE FIDEOS
ANGEL HAIR PASTA SOUP

The healthy aspect of Mexican cooking is happily linked to an abundance of carbohydrates in the form of tortillas, beans, rice and pasta. Mexican cooks probably use more fideos than any other pasta, the best being the tiniest, wirelike loops. The closest thing to fideos is angel hair pasta.

A dominant and unique aspect of true Mexican cooking is the custom of toasting ingredients. Rice and fideos are frequently toasted in oil as a first step thus adding flavor but more fat. I have found that the flavor can be retained by toasting the fideos in the oven minus the oil.

12 ounces of Mexican fideos or vermicelli
1 cup chopped onion
2 cups peeled, seeded tomatoes
(you can substitute canned plum tomatoes)
1 teaspoon minced garlic
2 quarts chicken stock (reduced sodium)
1 mild fresh green chile (Anaheim), chopped, seeded
1 teaspoon mild ground chile
(like Dixon or California)
1/4 cup grated Asiago or Parmesan cheese

Grind the onion, tomatoes, and garlic together in a food processor or chop by hand. Stir into the chicken stock. Bring to a simmer. Add the chopped green chile and the chile powder. Simmer for 15 minutes to blend flavors.

Break up the coils of fideos on a jelly roll pan and toast

PER SERVING:
233 calories
8 g protein
42 g carbohydrate
3 g fat
2 mg cholesterol
71 mg sodium

Note: you can find real fideos in Mexican grocery stores or order from Pendery's of Fort Worth, Texas. See Resources.

for about 8 to 10 minutes in a preheated 350 degree oven. Add the toasted fideos to the soup and simmer for 3 to 4 minutes. After ladling the soup into bowls, sprinkle tops with Parmesan cheese. I usually serve this soup with a warm tomato salsa that each person can stir into the soup for a more picante flavoring.

8 servings.

ME AND HUGO'S
CALDO DE TLALPEÑO

Have you ever eaten something in a restaurant and you knew by the second mouthful that you had to have the recipe? Most chefs protect their prize recipes but love to talk food. For concocting a soup, you don't need an exact recipe but knowing a rough assemblage of ingredients helps. One of the best Caldo de Tlapeño that I had tasted in or out of Mexico was Hugo's but he evaded all of my dumb questions with smart, dumb answers.

Forgive me, Hugo but you challenged me and I went after your soup. It was the ground, dried chipotle chile that threw me off momentarily because Hugo denied its existence. It's the most important ingredient in the soup because it adds the elusive smokiness necessary to this soup.

2 quarts chicken broth, see page 71 or 72
2 teaspoons oregano
1 pound red-skinned potatoes, halved

PER SERVING:
258 calories
23 g protein
23 g carbohydrate
8 g fat
49 mg cholesterol
99 mg sodium

Note: buy dried chipotle chiles in Mexican grocery store or send to Don Alfonso Foods. See Resources.

2 green bell peppers, cored and cut into chunks
2 stalks celery with leaves, sliced thickly
1 tomato, roasted under broiler, ground in blender
2 teaspoons mild ground chile
   (like California or pasilla)
1 to 2 teaspoons ground, dried chipotle chile
2 cups shredded cooked chicken breast,
   left from making chicken broth
1/2 cup green onion, chopped
2 cups fresh spinach, washed, stemmed, shredded
1/4 cup cilantro
1 ripe but firm avocado, skinned and sliced
Yellow Rice, stirred into soup at table

Put the stock in 4-quart pot and bring to a simmer; add oregano, potatoes, bell peppers, celery, pureed tomato, red chile, and chipotle powders. Cook the vegetables and stock for 25 minutes and then add the cooked chicken.

While soup is simmering, prepare the green onions, spinach, cilantro, and avocado. Just before serving stir it all into the soup so the spinach and green onions remain bright green. The avocado slices placed in the soup at the very last minute will also remain bright green. The warmth of the soup brings out the velvety taste of the avocado.

When you order Caldo de Tlapeño soup at Hugo's restaurant in Van Nuys, you can hear him chopping all this stuff back in the kitchen so he can add it to your soup bowl at the last minute. Hugo also gives you a little bowl of the Yellow Rice to add to your soup. Recipe below.

8 servings.

Note: you can use long-grain brown basmati rice in place of white rice. Simmer 2 and 1/2 cups water, 1 cup brown rice, 1/2 teaspoon salt and 1 teaspoon tumeric. Simmer on low for 40 minutes. Leave rice undisturbed for 10 minutes.

YELLOW RICE

PER SERVING:
94 calories
2 g protein
19 g carbohydrate
1 g fat
2 mg cholesterol
147 mg sodium

2 cups boiling water
1 cup long-grain white rice
2 teaspoons butter or margarine
1/2 teaspoon salt (Hugo uses more)
1 teaspoon tumeric powder

Bring water to a simmer and add the rice, butter, salt, and tumeric which will turn the rice gold like Hugo's. Turn heat to low and cook rice gently for 25 minutes. Do not peek. Turn off heat and still do not remove lid for 10 minutes. The rice will continue to steam. Place in a bowl, fluffing the rice with a fork. Each person adds a dollop of rice to a bowl of Caldo de Tlapeño and offers a blessing for Hugo's stubbornness and good soup.

8 servings of 1/4 cup each when adding to soup.

ENCHILADA SOUP

PER SERVING:
221 calories
12 g protein
34 g carbohydrate
5 g fat
10 mg cholesterol
220 mg sodium

A hearty, warming soup with a reminiscence of enchiladas. I often make this soup in the winter and when we come in from a chilling walk, Enchilada Soup is a welcome friend.

1/2 cup pinto beans
1/2 cup red beans or black beans
8 cups water
4 cloves garlic
2 onions, chopped
6 dried California or New Mexican chiles
2 corn tortillas, torn into small pieces
4 tomatoes, skins removed and chopped
    (2 and 1/2 cups)
1 teaspoon ground cumin
2 teaspoons oregano
1 tablespoon ground chile powder (like Dixon or
    California)
1 teaspoon Tabasco
1/2 cup sliced black olives
Olive oil mist
3 corn tortillas, cut into strips
1/4 pound reduced-fat Cheddar cheese, grated
2 tablespoon chives or chopped green onions
Salt to taste

Note: you can substitute store bought baked corn chips for the homemade tortilla strips.

Rinse beans and pick over for stones. Place 8 cups water with the chopped onion and garlic in a 3-quart pot. Simmer for 2 hours or until beans are tender yet firm.

While the beans are cooking wash off the dried chiles in cold water. Break apart and remove the large veins and seeds. Place the chiles in a 2-quart saucepan and cover with water. Simmer for 15 minutes. Remove and place in a blender with a cup of fresh water. Blend until pureed and then add the pieces of corn tortilla and tomatoes. Grind together.

When beans are cooked, drain off half of their cooking water and reserve; add chile-tomato puree, ground cumin, oregano, chile powder, and Tabasco. Simmer for 45 minutes. During the last 15 minutes, stir in the sliced black olives. If soup is too thick, add some of the reserved bean liquid.

Spray the olive oil on both sides of the tortilla strips and toast them on a baking sheet in a preheated 350 degree oven for about 10 minutes or until crisp and golden but not browned.

Taste for salt, adding from 1/2 teaspoon to 1 and 1/2 teaspoons. These amounts are optional and are not included in the nutritional analysis.

Ladle the Enchilada Soup over a few crisp tortilla strips placed in each bowl and sprinkle with some of the shredded cheese and chives. This is a very hearty and filling soup and you only need cold beer and some warm bolillos or tortillas to accompany it. If I have a couple of cups of this soup left I freeze it and then when I have leftover vegetable soup, I combine the two soups. If soup is too thick after refrigeration, thin it with reduced sodium chicken broth.

Serves 8.

SPICY SPLIT PEA SOUP

My husband thinks this is the best recipe for split pea that I've ever made, probably because I have indoctrinated him into believing that nothing is good without chile even split pea soup.

1 pound of split peas
8 cups water
2 cups chopped white onion
2 bay leaves
2 stalks celery with leaves, diced (1 cup)
The white part of 2 leeks, well-washed
    and diced (1 cup)
1 yam, peeled and diced
3 cloves garlic, minced
1 tablespoon fresh thyme
1 teaspoon oregano
2 teaspoons ground chile
1/4 teaspoon cinnamon
2 carrots, peeled and diced (1 cup)
1 ten-ounce package of frozen petite peas
Low fat milk, 1 cup for thinning soup

PER SERVING:
291 calories
18 g protein
53 g carbohydrate
2 g fat
2 mg cholesterol
105 mg sodium

Rinse the dried peas and then place in a 3-quart pot. Cover with water, onion, bay leaf, celery, leeks, yam, garlic, thyme, oregano, chile, and add one 2-inch stick canela (Mexican cinnamon). If you don't have canela, substitute with regular cinnamon. Simmer the soup for about 1 and a half to 2 hours.

Remove canela and bay leaves; puree soup in 3 batches in a blender ; I puree right in the soup pot using my hand held blender. I love this tool because you don't have to pour hot liquids back and forth.

After pureeing, add the diced carrots and baby peas. Simmer the soup and newly added vegetables for about 15 minutes or until the carrots are tender. If the soup seems too thick, thin it with the milk just before serving.

8 servings

SWEET POTATO AND JALAPEÑO SOUP

This soup is served at one of those very California restaurants along the coast and I loved it at my first mouthful. The original recipe used a lot of heavy cream which has been replaced with skim evaporated milk; there is no loss of flavor because of the rich taste of the sweet potatoes and carrots. For special occasions I add 2 to 4 tablespoons of real cream to the soup pot.

1 and 1/2 pounds sweet potatoes, peeled and diced
4 carrots, peeled and diced
6 cups chicken broth
1 teaspoon fresh thyme
2 teaspoons oil
1 cup chopped onion
2 jalapeño chiles, seeded and minced
2 teaspoons maple syrup
Pinch of cayenne pepper
12 ounces low fat evaporated milk (2%)

Simmer the sweet potatoes, carrots, broth, and the fresh thyme for 45 minutes or until they are very tender.

PER SERVING:
175 calories
5 g protein
30 g carbohydrate
4 g fat
8 mg cholesterol
73 mg sodium

In 2 teaspoons of oil saute the onion and chiles over very low heat, stirring frequently so they do not brown. In a blender puree the sweet potato-carrot mixture and the sautéed vegetables in batches; or add sauteed vegetables to the sweet potatoes and puree in pot using a hand held blender.

Season the soup with maple syrup, cayenne pepper, salt, and the milk. Blend with a whisk. Heat gently and serve in small bowls as a first course. If you could allow yourself the splurge, whisk in 1/4 cup of heavy cream just as you were finishing the soup. This amount of cream adds 2.75 grams of fat or 25 calories to each serving.

8 servings

Note: the restaurant added 1 and 1/2 cups heavy cream to enrich the soup!

TOASTED SOPA DE TORTILLA

This soup is very close to one enjoyed in the town of Patzcuaro, Mexico where we had gone for a restful holiday. We went back to the same restaurant on the square to eat Toasted Sopa de Tortilla every day.

Often in Mexico, the purer versions of tortilla soup have no vegetables but only crisp tortilla strips and some shreds of chicken floating in a chile broth. But typical of the Mexican kitchen, the ingredients are toasted to heighten the flavors.

8 cups chicken broth, see recipe on page 71 or use
*   reduced-sodium, fat-free canned broth*
6 ancho chiles
6 pasilla chiles
1 dried chipotle chile or mora chile
5 unpeeled cloves of garlic
1 onion
1 corn tortilla, quartered
4 tomatoes
Olive oil or canola oil mist
10 corn tortillas, cut into tiny strips
1 avocado, ripe but firm
1/2 cup Mexican fresh white cheese like queso
*   fresco, queso ranchero or reduced -fat Monterey*
*   Jack*

Using a cast-iron pan, toast the chiles over medium heat until they soften and give off a toasty aroma. DO NOT DARKEN the chiles, just toast them. It takes about 2 minutes; remove chiles from pan and cool. Cover with boiling water for 20 minutes. Remove chiles from hot water and simmer in the chicken broth.

Meanwhile using the same cast-iron pan, toast the unpeeled garlic cloves, the unpeeled onion, and the quartered tortilla. Toast garlic until it softens, about 20 minutes. Toast onion 20 minutes and tortilla for about 10 minutes or until it has black flecks. Add tortilla to the chicken-chile broth along with the roasted garlic and onion (from which you have removed the skins).

Roast the tomatoes for 20 minutes in a preheated 400 degree oven and place in the chicken-chile broth. Simmer this spicy soup base for 30 more minutes to meld flavors.

Puree the entire soup base (the chile-tomato-garlic mixture) in a blender or use hand held blender to puree right in the pot.

Mist the corn tortillas on both sides with olive oil spray. Cut into thin strips. Place the tortilla strips on a baking sheet and bake in a preheated 350 degree oven for about 10 minutes or until golden and crisp.

When serving the tortilla soup, pour into bowls and garnish with the crisp tortilla strips. Place avocado slices on the top. Pass the cheese for each person to add as garnish. Plan about 1 tablespoon per serving.

Serves 8.

MEXICAN VEGETABLE SALSA SOUP

I fix this soup when I have lived too well and just want vegetables. Perfect meal for a rich peasant with a fine loaf and a robust bottle.

10 cups liquid (water, stock, vegetable water)
1 cup tomato salsa, store bought or homemade
2 stalks celery with leaves, sliced
1/2 onion, chopped
2 cloves garlic, minced
1 teaspoon oregano
1 teaspoon sweet basil
4 carrots, sliced
Add 3 of the following vegetables:
1 cup green beans
1 cup sliced zucchini
1 cup corn kernels, fresh or frozen
1 cup of cubed red potatoes (or Russet)
1/2 cup frozen peas
1 cup of chayote, peeled and diced
1/2 cup rosamarinas (rice-shaped pasta) or macaroni

Combine all of the liquid, the salsa, and the vegetables of your choice. Simmer for 20 minutes. Then stir in the rosamarinas or macaroni and simmer for 10 more minutes.

8 servings.

PER SERVING:
105 calories
4 g protein
22 g carbohydrate
.6 g fat
0 mg cholesterol
74 mg sodium

Note: Since I concoct a lot of soups and freeze leftovers, one day I successfully combined leftover Mexican Vegetable Salsa Soup with Enchilada Soup. So now I try to have both soups in the freezer.
Also the Mexican Vegetable Salsa Soup done with corn, zucchini, and green beans is a good base for that old standby Sopa de Albóndigas. See recipe below for Albóndigas which are just small meatballs and add them to the vegetable soup. Also delete the pasta if you are doing the meatball soup.

ALBÓNDIGAS FOR SOUP

Often meatball soup is the only soup served in Mexican restaurants and it is often salty. You can make it so much better at home.

1/2 pound very lean ground beef (15%)
1/2 pound ground turkey (7% fat)
1/2 cup fresh bread crumbs, white or whole wheat
1/4 cup finely chopped onion
3 green chiles (canned is fine) chopped finely
1 clove garlic, minced through a press
2 tablespoons fresh mint, minced
1/2 cup parsley, minced
1/2 teaspoon ground cumin
1 teaspoon red chile
1/2 teaspoon salt

Mix together the ground beef, ground turkey, bread crumbs, onions, chiles, garlic, mint, parsley, cumin, red chile, and salt; form into small meatballs about the size of a walnut. Drop them into simmering soup (see recipe above) and cook over low heat with the lid on the pot for 20 minutes.

Serves 8. Makes 16 meatballs, 2 per person.

PER SERVING:
140 calories
11 g protein
7 g carbohydrate
7 g fat
40 mg cholesterol
241 mg sodium

Note: add these albóndigas (meatballs) to the Mexican Vegetable Salsa Soup for a more substantial meal. Add 2 to each bowl of soup.

TARASCAN BEAN SOUP

PER SERVING:
234 calories
12 g protein
42 g carbohydrate
3 g fat
0 mg cholesterol
274 mg sodium

This soup from the state of Michoacan, Mexico is one of the most delicate of Mexican soups. Because of the rich taste of pinto beans, it is unnecessary to add more than the small amount of olive oil for sautéing the vegetables.

By completely pureeing the beans, the smoothness of the soup maximizes the gentle flavors. When I first tested this recipe, I pureed only enough beans to thicken the broth; for the second test I pureed everything. What a difference it made. My husband thought that it was a different soup.

A sister to this soup is a regular every Saturday at the famous El Mirador in San Antonio, Texas.

12 ounces pinto beans
6 cups water
2 ancho chiles, torn in half
1 onion, chopped roughly
3 cloves garlic, minced
4 tomatoes, broiled
1 onion with skins on, cut in half
4 cloves garlic
1 tablespoon olive oil
1 teaspoon ground cumin
1 teaspoon oregano
3 cups chicken broth (reduced sodium)
2 ancho chiles
4 corn tortillas, cut into strips

Rinse the beans in a sieve, picking through them for stones. Place in a large pot and cover with water. Bring to a simmer, cook for 3 minutes, and then allow the beans to stand in the liquid for at least 2 hours. Drain off this soaking water and discard.

Add 6 cups of fresh water to the drained beans along with the ancho chile pieces, onion, and garlic. I like to use my pressure cooker for beans because it shortens the time needed for cooking. If using a pressure cooker, cook for 45 minutes. If you are using a regular pot, simmer the beans for about 1 and 1/2 hours or until tender.

Meanwhile, prepare the rest of the soup. Place the tomatoes, onion, and garlic in a pie pan and broil just until the tomato skins blister and brown. Turn the tomatoes over once. This should take about 5 minutes total. When cool enough to handle, skin the tomatoes and squeeze out the seeds. Remove the skins from the onion and garlic. Place everything in a food processor and puree roughly. Heat the oil in a 3-quart pot and add the tomato-onion puree; simmer for 10 minutes, adding the cumin and oregano. Set aside.

Note: the taste of ancho chiles has often been compared to that of a spicy raisin. Pendery's of Texas has soft, sweet ancho chiles, See Resources.

In a food processor (the same processor bowl used for pureeing the tomatoes) puree the beans, their liquid, and the ancho chiles. It is best to do this in three batches.

Add each batch of bean puree to the pot with the tomato-onion mixture. Stir 2 cups of chicken broth into bean soup to thin ; add more broth if necessary. Simmer for 15 minutes. Watch carefully since puree burns easily. Taste for salt and add 1/2 teaspoon to 1 and 1/2 teaspoons. This amount is not included in the nutritional analysis.

Mist the tortillas with olive oil mist or canola oil. Cut into strips and toast for 8 minutes in a preheated 350 degree oven until they are crisp but not browned.

At the same time you are toasting tortilla strips, place the ancho chiles in a pie plate and toast for 8 minutes. Crumble the chile and serve it sprinkled over the top of each serving of soup along with the homemade tortilla chips.

8 servings.

BLACK BEAN SOUP WITH MARINATED RICE

Black beans, traditional fare in the Caribbean, Yucatan, and Cuba, seem to be found in everything from chips to salads to chili these days. From the very first time I tasted black bean soup in Merida, Yucatan I was hooked. I have played with this recipe a great deal in my own kitchen finally settling on this one as my very favorite.

1 pound black beans
8 cups water
1 ham bone or 4 ounces of lean ham (96% fat free)
1 onion, half
3 cloves garlic
3 bay leaves
Cooked black beans from above
3 cloves garlic
1 onion, peeled and quartered
1 chipotle chile en adobo from can
1 to 2 cups fat-free reduced-sodium chicken broth

PER SERVING:
298 calories
16 g protein
53 g carbohydrate
3 g fat
73 mg cholesterol
519 mg sodium

1 teaspoon salt
Marinated rice:
1 and 1/2 cups cooked rice
1/3 cup minced onion
1 tablespoon olive oil
3 tablespoons vinegar 1/2 teaspoon freshly ground
   black pepper

If you want the beans to remain wonderfully pitch black, you cannot presoak them with the hot water method. Just put the beans in a sieve and rinse them off. Place in a pot, cover with 8 cups of water, the ham bone, onion, garlic, and bay leaves. Bring to a boil and then simmer for about 1 and 1/2 hours on low heat. The ham will add some salt so taste the beans before you add more salt.

While the beans are cooking, wrap up the onion, garlic and chipotle chile in foil; bake at 350 degrees for 40 minutes.

Puree the beans, their liquid, (reserve the cooked ham bone for another use) and the roasted onion-garlic in batches in a blender. Leave some of the beans whole for more texture. If the soup is too thick, thin with chicken broth using about 1/4 cup at a time until the soup is of the desired consistency.

Combine the cooked rice, onion, olive oil, vinegar, and pepper. Set aside until you serve the soup. This velvety soup is topped with a tablespoon of marinated rice for each serving. You may also pass lime wedges, sherry, or bottled hot sauce to be added at the table.

8 servings.

EASY MEXICAN GAZPACHO

I have lightened the gazpacho recipe from my *California Rancho Cooking* and made it easier, spicier, and with less olive oil than traditionally called for. You will need less olive oil if you use one with great flavor.

PER SERVING:
87 calories
3 g protein
17 g carbohydrate
2 g fat
0 mg cholesterol
864 mg sodium

2 cloves garlic
1/2 red onion or mild onion (about 1 cup)
1 cucumber, peeled
Juice from 1 lemon
2 tablespoons red wine vinegar
1 can Italian plum tomatoes, drained
1/2 teaspoon hot pepper sauce
1 tablespoon virgin olive oil
1/2 teaspoon freshly ground pepper
1/2 teaspoon salt
1 tablespoon fresh sweet basil or 1 teaspoon dried
3 tablespoon cilantro, snipped with scissors
4 cups spicy or regular tomato juice
Gazpacho vegetables for adding to soup
1 English cucumber, peeled and diced
4 green onion, minced
2 fresh tomatoes, diced

Plan to make the gazpacho at least two hours before you need it so the flavors may season. In a blender, place the garlic, onion, cucumber, lemon juice, vinegar, plum tomatoes, hot pepper sauce, olive oil, pepper, salt, sweet basil, and cilantro. Add 1 cup of the tomato juice. Puree to a smooth texture.

Pour into a 2-quart glass bowl and stir in the rest of the spicy tomato juice; stir in the diced cucumber, green onions, and tomatoes. Chill for 2 hours before serving.

Serves 8.

SOPA DE MAÍZ

Corn soup is just one of the ways in which an ingredient such as maíz (native corn) is treated very delicately. When this soup is made in Mexico, the thick crema doble is stirred into the soup to finish it off. In our version the pureed vegetables help fool our palates into thinking of cream. Also, the potatoes help to thicken the soup.

PER SERVING:
182 calories
7 g protein
36 g carbohydrate
3 g fat
6 mg cholesterol
439 mg sodium

2 packages (1 pound each) frozen sweet corn kernels
  or 6 cups fresh corn kernels
2 cups cubed, peeled Russet potatoes
3 cups chicken broth (fat-free and reduced-sodium)
2 teaspoons butter or olive oil
1 cup chopped onion
1 cup low-fat milk
2 teaspoons sugar
1 teaspoon salt (optional)
1 red bell pepper
1 green chile (Anaheim or poblano)
1 teaspoon red chile

Simmer the corn kernels and the potatoes in the chicken stock for 20 minutes.

Meanwhile sauté the onion in the butter for 8 minutes or until softened. Add to the corn and potatoes above.

Puree the corn-potato mixture in blender or puree in the pot using a hand held blender. Pour puree back into the cooking pot and stir milk, sugar, and salt into the soup.

Roast the red pepper and the green chile pepper under a boiler until blackened. Remove stems, seeds, and skins and chop the peppers. Add to the corn soup. Simmer the soup for 10 minutes, stirring frequently so it doesn't stick as purees are prone to do. Just before serving sprinkle with red chile.

8 servings.

MEXICAN SEAFOOD

CHAPTER IV

MEXICAN SEAFOOD DISHES

In the coastal villages of Mexico, seafood is treated with great respect and fondness. Some of our most memorable meals were prepared by fishermen on whose small boats we spent the day, off the small island, Isla de Mujeres. On the Yucatán Peninsula it is customary to barbecue fish over palmetto twigs rather than the chunks of mesquite used in other parts of Mexico.

When barbecuing or grilling fish, never place the fish over a fiercely hot barbecue. When our captain-fisher-man-cook barbecued a butterflied mero (sea bass) on the beach, the palmetto coals were smoldering so gently I thought the fire was dead until I held my hand over it.

Along the beach in Mexico, you can quickly fashion a grill out of green sticks but in your own backyard, the best fish grill is one of those hinged grills that you find in hardware stores or chain drugstores. The price is usually under $10. These grills are perfect for filets and butterflied fish because you can turn the fish without stabbing at it with a spatula. Before placing the fish inside, mist or rub the grill with oil.

Lastly, when barbecuing or grilling fish, be overzeal-ous about watching it as you stand by the fire with a cool libation.When my husband barbecues anything, he puts the meat over the fire and then leaves to paint the garage, returning to find a relic only suitable for Carbon 14 dating. Avid barbecuers or asadors nurse their fires, their wood, their marinades, their meats, their glasses of wine until they have created theater around the barbecue itself. Anything outside of that is immaterial.

GRILLED YUCATÁN FISH

In Yucatán, sea bass is often rubbed with a marinade of sour orange juice, lime juice, oil, and achiote paste I use a canned chipotle chile en adobo because it is easier to find. The chipotle's smokiness matches well with anything grilled particularly fish.

1 and 1/2 pounds sea bass, rock cod, or red snapper
*   filets*
1/4 cup lime juice
1/2 cup orange juice
1 teaspoon grated orange peel
1 tablespoon olive oil
1 teaspoon minced garlic
1 chipotle en adobo from can
1 tablespoon adobo juice from can
1/4 cup minced cilantro

Simmer the lime juice, orange juice, peel, olive oil, garlic, chipotle, and adobo juice for 10 minutes to concentrate flavors. Stir in the cilantro. Cool and then pour over fish, allowing it to marinate for 30 minutes.

Broil or grill fish for 5 to 7 minutes per side depending upon the thickness of the filets. Stick a fork into the middle of the filet and if it pulls away easily, almost flaking, the fish is done. Serve the grilled fish with a salad. If we ate like this all the time, our skin would glow.

Serves 6.

PER SERVING:
128 calories
18 g protein
4 g carbohydrate
4 g fat
39 mg cholesterol
139 mg sodium

Note: I have used this same marinade over whole, cleaned squid and then grilled them on an oiled barbecue for about 2 minutes per side. Sliced into rings they make a great appetizer while you are standing by the barbecue.

BAJA CALIFORNIA FISH TACOS

PER SERVING:
270 calories
24 g protein
29 g carbohydrate
6 g fat
35 mg cholesterol
236 mg sodium

In the seaport villages of Mexico, there are innumerable variations on the theme of fish tacos. Sometimes the fish is battered and deep-fried; sometimes it is boiled and flaked; or my personal favorite, grilled over a brazier of smoky mesquite. The taco shack on the beach offers you a variety of condiments from sliced radishes and lettuce to thinly-sliced white cabbage.

Even if you are not going to make tacos, this is a great marinade for fish or chicken you want to grill or barbecue.

1/4 cup lime juice
1 tablespoon olive oil
1 teaspoon minced garlic
1 chipotle chile en adobo from can
2 teaspoons adobo juice from can
1 and 1/2 pounds red snapper, rock cod, or shark filets
1/2 cup chopped onion
1/4 cup snipped cilantro
2 cups of chopped iceberg or romaine lettuce
Salsa, use good bottled or make recipe below
12 fresh corn tortillas

Blend together the lime juice, olive oil, garlic, chipotle chile. Add a little juice from the chipotle can for extra flavor. Rub this mixture all over the fish filets (or boned chicken or turkey) Marinate for at least 20 minutes.

Broil the fish filets 6 inches under a hot broiler for 3 minutes on each side. The exact timing will depend upon the thickness of the filets. When a fork is stuck into the filet, it should barely flake. You want it to remain moist. You can also place fish inside an oiled, hinged grill and barbecue over medium hot coals.

To prepare fish tacos, cut the filets into chunks and add chopped onion and cilantro. Warm the corn tortillas by wrapping them in foil and placing them in a preheated 350 degree oven for about 10 minutes or heat them on a comal or on the barbecue grill. Wrap the warm tortillas in a tea towel.

Everyone spoons some of the fish-cilantro mixture into a soft tortilla and adds salsa and lettuce. Lucy's Salsa and the Lime-Jalapeño Salsa are great with Fish Tacos.

Serves 6

LUCY'S HOT SALSA

In October we drive to the Tehachapi mountains for fresh apples and an early breakfast at a little diner frequented by the local folk. Lucy makes this salsa just for the diner and it is kept on each table in one of the plastic squeeze bottles, looking sort of lethal green (because she adds more jalapeños). Locally, it is liberally sprinkled over everything but the pancakes.

1 can ready-cut, peeled tomatoes including juices
   (28 ounces)
4 or 5 jalapeño chiles, leaving some seeds
1 tablespoon minced garlic
1/2 cup diced red onion
1/4 teaspoon salt
2 teaspoons vinegar
1/4 cup minced cilantro

PER SERVING:
27 calories
1 g protein
6 g carbohydrate
.3 g fat
0 mg cholesterol
230 mg sodium

When tomatoes in the store are pink and hard, make this salsa. The canned tomatoes (S & W makes the ready-cut type) are the closest you can get to good fresh ones. Put the tomatoes and their juices into the bowl of a food processor. Add jalapeños(cut into pieces), garlic, red onion, salt, and vinegar. Chop to a coarse puree.

Simmer the salsa in an open saucepan for 10 minutes to concentrate the flavors. After you remove the salsa from the heat, stir in the cilantro. Taste to see if you need to add more salt.

Makes about 3 and 1/2 cups or 8 servings

JALAPEÑO LIME SALSA

This salsa has the earthy flavor of charred chiles as the blackened skins are left on for the salsa.

5 jalapeño chiles
1 clove minced garlic
Juice of 4 limes (1/2 cup)
2 teaspoons olive oil
1/2 teaspoon salt
2 tablespoons minced cilantro

Char the jalapeño chiles by holding over the gas flame of your stove or placing them under a broiler. Turn until they are evenly charred. Remove stems but keep the seeds. Mince chiles, including the charred skins. Combine with garlic, lime juice, olive oil, salt, and cilantro.

PER SERVING:
1 TABLESPOON
15 calories
0 g protein
2 g carbohydrate
1 g fat
0 mg cholesterol
107 mg sodium

MEXICAN CEVICHE SALAD

Because so many people are hesitant to eat raw fish, I prepare my recipe for Mexican ceviche using barely poached scallops so it resembles the conch salads served in the Caribbean and Yucatán.

Heaped in a huge shell, it makes a wonderful appetizer when served with either warm corn tortillas or slices from a baguette.

1 pound large scallops
1 bottle clam juice
Juice from 1 lemon
1/2 cup red bell pepper, diced
2 tomatoes, diced
1/2 cup red onion, diced
1 jalapeño chile, seeds removed, diced
Juice of 3 limes
Juice of 1 orange
1 to 2 tablespoons olive oil
1/2 teaspoon dried oregano
2 tablespoons cilantro, snipped with scissors
Freshly ground pepper to taste

Bring clam juice and lemon juice to a simmer and add the scallops. Bring to a gentle simmer and poach the scallops for just 2 minutes so they are just barely cooked. Do not walk away from the stove. Drain the scallops and cool. Chop finely.

Combine the diced bell pepper, tomatoes, onion, and jalapeño chile.

PER SERVING:
115 calories
13 g protein
7 g carbohydrate
3 g fat
25 mg cholesterol
147 mg sodium

To the warm scallops, add the lime and orange juice, the olive oil, oregano, cilantro, and pepper. Stir in the diced vegetables. Let the salad marinate for at least 2 hours before serving.

Serves 6 as an appetizer.

RED SNAPPER FILETS VERACRUZ STYLE

During the five years we lived in central Mexico it was easy to get a good steak but difficult to obtain seafood, thereby only increasing our cravings for it.

Our Mexican compadre, Eduardo, convinced us one Christmas vacation to spend a couple of weeks overdosing on seafood in the coastal town of Veracruz.

Every morning we sat under the portales and ate whole huachinango (red snapper) fried in butter for breakfast . For mid-morning repast, tall glasses of cafe con leche and toasted bolillos were eaten at La Parroquia while we were teased by 6-year olds selling lottery tickets. Then it was on to shrimp and oysters for lunch; for dinner, our most requested dish was huachinango veracruzano.

After two weeks of this regimen, we were cured for awhile and ready to resume our highland diet back in Querétaro where the closest thing to the sea was canned tuna.

Most often, in Mexico the red snapper is cooked whole in all of its glory but the filets cooked in the same traditional sauce used for huachinango are quite wonderful and less trouble for the cook.

6 red snapper or rock cod filets, about 4 ounces each
2 teaspoons olive oil
1 can plum tomatoes and their juices (28 ounces)
1 cup chopped onion
1 teaspoon minced garlic
2 teaspoons red ground chile
1/8 teaspoon canela or cinnamon
1/2 teaspoon sugar
2 teaspoons lemon juice
1 tablespoon orange juice
1/4 cup pimiento stuffed olives
1/4 cup pickled jalapeño chiles, sliced
Lemon or lime slices for garnish
Chopped parsley or cilantro for garnish

Heat the olive oil and saute the onion and garlic until softened and then add the tomatoes, drained and chopped. Stir in the canela, sugar, lemon juice, orange juice, stuffed olives, and pickled jalapeños. Simmer for about 15 minutes.

Preheat oven to 350 degrees. Place 1 cup sauce on bottom of an oiled baking dish. Lay filets on top and cover with the rest of the sauce. Bake for 20 minutes and then check to see if fish barely flakes. If they are thick filets, they may need as much as 5 minutes longer.

Serve the fish in the baking dish garnished with the sauce, lemon or lime slices, and chopped cilantro or parsley. Accompany with simple steamed rice or steamed new potatoes.

Serves 6.

MICHAEL GRANT'S BOUILLABAISSE CHILI

PER SERVING:
329 calories
37 g protein
13 g carbohydrate
14 g fat
87 mg cholesterol
615 mg sodium

Whenever I serve this chili I have immediate requests for the recipe. If anyone was going to be sacrilegious about a chili dish, it might as well be a Texan as Texan as Michael, a columnist for the San Diego Union.

16 medium shrimp
1 can tomato sauce, 8 ounces
1 can tomato juice, 12 ounces
1 bottle clam juice, 8 ounces
3 red bell peppers
3 fresh Anaheim chiles
2 fresh jalapeño chiles
2 and 1/2 tablespoons cumin seeds
3 bay leaves
2 teaspoons olive oil
1 cup celery, chopped
1 cup onion, chopped
6 cloves garlic, minced through a press
1 tablespoon good chile powder (like Dixon)
2 teaspoons black pepper
Salt to taste
1 pound red snapper fillets, cut into 2-inch pieces
1 pound halibut, cut into 2-inch pieces
1/2 pound bay scallops
12 fresh mussels, bearded and scrubbed (optional)
1 to 2 cups water
1 bunch cilantro

Peel and vein the shrimp. Combine tomato sauce, tomato juice, clam juice and shrimp shells in a saucepan and simmer 15 minutes to create a delicious stock.

Under a broiler, roast the peppers and chiles until the skins are black all over. Steam the peppers and chiles in a paper bag for 5 minutes, then peel and seed them, and in a blender on low speed, reduce them to pulp.

Strain the shells from the tomato juice mixture, add the pureed peppers and chiles to the tomato juice, and continue to simmer. Toast the cumin seeds in a hot, dry skillet until golden and fragrant. Crush the seeds and bay leaves in an electric coffee grinder. I have one reserved just for spices.

Cut the fish fillets into 2-inch pieces. In a 6-quart pot, fry the vegetables and garlic in olive oil. Add the spices and fry 1 minute, stirring constantly. Add the fish and shellfish and tomato-pepper mixture, and enough water to cover. Keep the stew on a low steady boil for 15 minutes. Add chopped cilantro during the last 5 minutes. Serve in large bowls with crusty French bread or fresh Mexican Bolillos. Sometimes when you prepare this it is difficult to find one of the fish or in particular, the fresh mussels. In this case, double up on the scallops or substitute something like squid. The last time I made the bouillabaisse I found beautiful, cleaned Monterey squid. I just sliced the squid into rings and added it during the last 6 minutes of cooking and it was quite tender.

8 servings

BLACK BEAN SEAFOOD CHILI

PER SERVING:
388 calories
45 g protein
34 g carbohydrate
6 g fat
107 mg cholesterol
746 mg sodium

This chili is a delicious surprise for anyone used to traditional chili with beef. You can add a variety of firm fish and shellfish depending upon availability in your area.

1 tablespoon olive oil
1 cup diced onions
1/2 cup roasted, peeled, and seeded Anaheim chiles
1 cup diced red bell pepper
1 cup fresh corn kernels, sliced off the cob
2 tablespoons minced garlic (yes!)
1 jalapeño chile, seeded and minced
1 to 2 tablespoons pureed chipotle en adobo
1 teaspoon ground cumin
2 teaspoons red chile
1 teaspoon dried oregano
2 cups peeled, diced tomatoes
2 cups cooked black beans, see page 16
2 cups fish or chicken stock
1/2 cup white wine
1 pound sea scallops, well-rinsed
1 pound firm fish like halibut or rock cod, diced
1/2 pound bay shrimp
Salt and pepper to taste
1/4 cup minced cilantro for garnish

Sauté onions, bell pepper, and green chile in the olive oil and then stir in the corn, garlic, jalapeño, and chipotle puree. Add cumin, red chile, oregano, and diced tomato.

Simmer for 30 minutes to blend flavors and then stir in the cooked black beans. Cook for another 5 minutes.

Heat stock and white wine. When simmering stir in the scallops and halibut. Cook just until they turn white, just a couple of minutes. Now ladle the scallops, fish, and bay shrimp and all but 1 cup of stock into the pot holding the chili. Very gently combine so as not to break up the seafood. If the chile needs more liquid, add the last cup of stock. Taste for seasoning, adding salt and pepper to your taste. Serve in shallow bowls garnished with cilantro.

Serves 6.

THE HOLY TRINITY

CHAPTER V

THE HOLY TRINITY OF THE SOUTHWEST
AND NEW VERSIONS OF TRADITIONAL RECIPES

hat has been practiced in the Southwest since antiquity, is now recognized as healthful; the culinary trinity of **beans, corn, and chiles** are as necessary to the true native diet as air and water to survival. One element rarely exists without the other. Vegetables are often merely seasoned with meats while large servings of meats and fowl are reserved for feast days and Sundays. Unfortunately, as with Mexican cooking, many traditional Southwestern recipes are laden with pork and lard. The patriarchs of many families have been told to cut out or decrease fat intake.

Even all the healthy beans and chiles cannot prevail against a high intake of fat. The fat, especially lard, adds a unique flavor and an unctuousness to the food. Tamales made with half their weight in lard are creamier; pozole with the pork shoulder and pig's feet is richer in flavor; the tacos and Indian fry bread cooked in bubbly lard are crisper. Perhaps, for an occasional feast day or birthday dinner, the old food will always be there but for everyday, we all need to seriously cut back on the amount of hidden fat that works its way into our diets and seriously affects long-term health.

I do not wish to throw out the traditional foods but I am allowing the cooking trinity to de-emphasize the importance of fat and our reliance on it for flavor.

Beans, the First of the Trinity

Historically, beans have been important for subsistence in many places at many times. My Spanish-Californian grandmother fed five hungry children on beans and tortillas.

Many people are hungry for down-home foods and beans (along with lumpy mashed potatoes) are enjoying a gastronomic renaissance that tops all comfort food. Bean varieties, many of ancient stock, are now available at health food stores and through mail order. I am tantalized by the old names—anasazi, ojo de cabra, flor de mayo, tepary, and azufrado. If you send away for freshly harvested beans, from ranches or the Native Seeds Search in Tucson, you will be amazed at how quickly fresh, dried beans cook and how marvelous they taste.

The facts about beans make a good case for their health value: they average about 120 calories per half a cup and that amount will give you enough fiber to equal a bowl of oatmeal or a medium oat bran muffin.

When beans are combined with pasta, rice, or other complex carbohydrates, they form a complete protein. Through the ages, it is obvious that combinations such as red beans and rice of Louisiana and tortillas and beans of Hispanic cultures were instinctively wise.

DYNAMITE VEGETARIAN CHILI

This chili recipe is so outstanding I urge you to banish any preconceived notions about vegetarian cooking. Carnivores are mad about this chile. The real secret to great chile is to use the best ground chile powders with superb flavor such as Dixon and Chimayo from New Mexico. Toast spices such as the cumin seed and oregano leaves to enhance their flavors even more. Because of the combination of the beans, the bulgur, and the tofu, this chili packs a high amount of nutrients and would be a perfect food for discriminating marathoners.

PER SERVING:
527 calories
28 g protein
98 g carbohydrate
6 g fat
0 mg cholesterol
533 mg sodium

1 pound anasazi beans (or pinto is okay)
8 cups water
1 onion, chopped
2 cloves garlic, minced
1 tablespoon cumin seed
1 tablespoon dried oregano leaves
2 teaspoons olive oil
3 cups chopped onion (about 2 onions)
1 tablespoon minced garlic
2 cups chopped red bell pepper (1 large pepper)
1 cup chopped green bell pepper (1 small pepper)
4 jalapeño chiles, seeded, minced
2 cans Italian plum tomatoes (28 ounces each)
1/4 cup ground chile like New Mexican Dixon
10.5 ounces of tofu (Mori-Nu), frozen and thawed
1/2 cup bulgur (cracked wheat)
2 cups corn niblets, canned or frozen

Note: more water is required for cooking unsoaked beans while presoaked beans can be cooked in 6 cups water.

Rinse beans in sieve under running water. Check for stones. Place in 3-quart pot and cover with 8 cups water. Because the beans turn out so creamy, I prefer covering them with water, the chopped onion and garlic and pressure-cooking them for 45 minutes. If you do not have a pressure cooker, simmering the beans in a pot will take approximately 2 hours.

While the beans are cooking, prepare the rest of the chile. Toast the cumin seed in a heavy skillet just until there is a slight change of color, about 2 minutes. Add the oregano to the same skillet and toast for about a minute. Mash the seeds and oregano in a mortar or a spice grinder.

Heat the olive oil in a large skillet and add the garlic and onion, sautéing just until softened. Next add the red and green bell peppers, and jalapeños. Puree drained plum tomatoes.

When the beans are cooked, stir in pureed tomatoes, the sautéed vegetables, the toasted cumin, oregano, and the chile powder. Simmer for 45 minutes to an hour.

Squeeze out the excess liquid from the thawed tofu. By freezing and then thawing, the tofu crumbles more easily and blends well into sauces. Crumble the tofu and stir into the pot of simmering chile. At first, it will resemble grated Parmesan cheese and then it will start to take on the red of the chile. Add the bulgur at the same time. Simmer for 35 more minutes. Taste to adjust for seasonings. Add the corn during the last 15 minutes of simmering.

Serves 6.

Note: you can find anasazi beans in health food stores. These beans have wonderful flavor and cook in half the time as pintos.

BASIC SIMPLE BEANS AS A FOUNDATION FOR RECIPES

Use these beans as a base for other recipes, like the ones that follow, or when you want simplicity itself. A simple pot of beans goes well with barbecue or my personal favorite, corn bread.

PER SERVING:
244 calories
17 g protein
37 g carbohydrate
3 g fat
106 mg cholesterol
411 mg sodium

1 pound beans, any type
2 teaspoons olive oil
1 chopped onion
2 teaspoons minced garlic
1 ham bone or 8 ounces Cajun tasso
1 teaspoon black pepper

Rinse beans in sieve, checking for stones. Place in pot and cover with water. Bring to boil. Boil for 3 minutes and turn off heat. Soak for 1 hour and pour off soaking water.

Put beans back into pot with 6 cups fresh water, sautéed onion, garlic, and Cajun tasso if you have it or the ham bone. Simmer for 2 hours. Add pepper and taste for salt.

6 servings.

BLACK BEAN CHILI AU GRATIN

If I was forced to choose my favorite between the Dynamite Vegetarian Chili or the Black Bean Chili, I could not. As often happens, I choose my favorite that day by what I have in the cupboard or refrigerator.

I have found that suppressed carnivores particularly love this chile because the golden crust of cheese satisfies their need for succulence. The three different types of chiles add a marvelous dimension to the black beans.

Note: tasso is a great tasting, lean Cajun spicy ham. Its peppery crust comes from the cayenne it's dusted with. The San Francisco sausage king, Bruce Aidells makes tasso. Small pieces can add flavor without adding excessive fat. See Resources for ordering info.

PER SERVING:
344 calories
21 g protein
52g carbohydrate
7 g fat
13 mg cholesterol
1128 mg sodium

5 cups cooked black beans and their liquid, (see
*   recipe on page 121*
2 teaspoons olive oil
1 and 1/2 cups chopped red onion
1 tablespoon minced garlic
2 bay leaves
1 sprig epazote (optional)
1 tablespoon cumin seed, toasted
2 teaspoons oregano, toasted
1/2 cup canned, pickled jalapeño chiles, chopped
1 canned chipotle en adobo, minced
1/2 cup tomato puree, like Pomi
6 dried red chiles (New Mexico or California)
1/4 pound grated reduced-fat Jack cheese

Follow recipe given for cooking beans on previous page. While the beans are cooking, sauté the chopped onions in the olive oil for 5 minutes. Add the garlic, bay leaves, and epazote during the last couple of minutes. In a separate small pan, toast the cumin seeds over medium heat and then add the oregano. Remove the pan from the heat. The residual heat of the pan will bring out the flavor of the oregano. Add the spices to the onion. Also add the pickled jalapeño chiles and the chipotle chile. Sauté all these ingredients together for about 5 more minutes and then stir into the beans when they are finished cooking.

Soak the dried chiles in boiling water for 30 minutes. Then place chiles in a blender jar, adding 1/2 cup fresh water (soaking water is often bitter). Puree until smooth. Add chile puree and the tomato puree to the pot of beans.

Simmer the Black Bean Chili for 45 minutes longer without a lid so the broth thickens and the flavors meld.

To serve, place chili in heatproof bowls and sprinkle each one with about 1/4 cup of grated cheese. Place all of the bowls on a jelly roll pan and slide under a preheated broiler. Broil until the cheese is bubbly and has developed a golden crust.

Serves 6.

BLACK BEAN PANCAKES

PER SERVING:
Each pancake
135 calories
5 g protein
19 g carbohydrate
4 g fat
3 mg cholesterol
153 mg sodium

There are still surprises left in life and these can stand up and be counted. Bean pancakes were not invented by nouvelle chefs but by my grandmother who always had leftover beans. She would heat up her cast-iron pan with about a 1/2-inch of olive oil and drop in a cup of beans, mashing them and sizzling them at the same time. The beans eventually became pancakes, crisp and golden around the edges and still creamy in the center.

My bean pancakes are an embellishment of Grandmama's minus a lot of olive oil. They are quite delicious with just a salad or quesadillas or even barbecued meats.

2 cups of cooked, drained black beans, use canned
  beans or see recipe, page 121
1 clove garlic, minced
2 teaspoon olive oil
1 bunch green onion, minced
1 canned, pickled jalapeño chile, minced
1 teaspoon red chile powder
1/2 teaspoon cumin seed, toasted and crushed
3/4 cup steamed barley (see procedure below)
2 tablespoon cilantro, snipped
2 tablespoons olive oil
1 cup of cornmeal or oat bran for coating
1/2 cup reduced-fat sour cream
Salsa for a topping

Puree only 1/2 cup of the beans and stir in the remaining whole beans. Mash everything together. Sauté the green onions in the 2 teaspoons of olive oil for 5 minutes. Add to the beans along with the jalapeño chile, chile powder, and cumin

You can make the pancakes without the barley if your bean mixture is fairly stiff. The day I was testing this recipe there was leftover steamed barley in the refrigerator. I liked its nuttiness and texture so I added some to the bean mixture. To steam barley, bring 2 and 1/2 cups of chicken broth or water to a simmer and add one cup of dried barley and 1/2 teaspoon of salt. Steam for about 30 minutes on low heat or until all of the liquid is absorbed.

Stir the cooked barley and the cilantro into the black bean mixture.

Place the cornmeal or oat bran on a piece of wax paper. Spoon 1/4 cup of the bean mixture onto the coating of your choice and use a spoon to turn it over, flattening it into a patty. Heat the oil, preferably in a nonstick skillet, and add 3 pancakes. Sauté about 2 minutes on each side and until golden brown. Turn over using a wide spatula. If you need more oil in the skillet, add only 1 teaspoon at a time. Serve each pancake with a teaspoon of low fat sour cream and some salsa.

Makes about 12 to 14 pancakes as an accompaniment to a dinner or lunch.

NAVAHO BEAN SALAD

PER SERVING:
201 calories
8 g protein
28 g carbohydrate
7 g fat
0 mg cholesterol
193 mg sodium

This bean salad was inspired by a superb, small book called *Pueblo and Navaho Cookery* by Marcia Keegan. I have lightened the dressing and added the cactus. Perfect for a summer barbecue, this salad is a welcome change from the generic, overly sweet bean salads. I often use one of the unusual native beans such as the brown tepary bean or the anasazi which cooks in half the time as the pinto. If you are pressed for time, you could use canned pinto or black beans, well-rinsed of their salty brine.

2 cups cooked pinto beans
2 cups cooked baby lima beans (frozen)
1 cup cooked green beans
2 cups cooked cactus (nopales) strips from jar, diced
1 and 1/2 cups sliced onion or bunch of green onions
2 teaspoons minced garlic
1 and 1/2 cups diced red bell pepper
1 teaspoon Dijon mustard
1 teaspoon sugar
1/4 teaspoon salt
1 teaspoon chile powder
1/4 cup oil
1/3 cup vinegar
1 teaspoon mild ground red chile
    (for sprinkling on top)

Mix all the vegetables together in a large bowl and then mix the dressing of mustard, sugar, salt, chile, oil, and vinegar. Toss the vegetables with the dressing and marinate for at least 2 hours. Before serving sprinkle the red chile on top for color.

Serves 8 as a side dish.

LENTIL CHILI

Lentils can quickly go from tiny ovals of texture to mush. The solution is to cook the sauce and lentils separately since the sauce needs more lengthy simmering. Then combine lentils and sauce for the final stage of cooking.

2 teaspoons oil
1 and 1/2 cups chopped onion
1 cup chopped celery (2 stalks)
1 cup chopped carrots (2)
1 cup chopped green pepper
1 tablespoon minced garlic
3/4 cup minced green onions
1/2 pound ground turkey
    (7% fat) optional but great
1 and 1/2 cups peeled, chopped tomatoes
1 can tomato paste, 6 ounces
3 cups water
1/2 teaspoon ground cumin
1 teaspoon oregano
3 tablespoons ground red chile
1 cup dry lentils
3 cups water
1/2 teaspoon salt
1 cup peeled, diced jicama

Place the oil in a 3-quart pot and fry the chopped onion, celery, carrots, green pepper, garlic, and green onions until softened. Set vegetables aside and fry the ground turkey until the meat loses it pink color. Add the sautéed vegetables back to the pan along with the tomatoes, tomato paste, water, cumin, oregano, and red chile. Simmer for 45 minutes.

Rinse the lentils in a sieve and then simmer in 3 cups of water for 25 minutes. Drain off the cooking water and add lentils to the tomato mixture. Simmer the Lentil Chili for 15 minutes and then stir in the diced jicama. Simmer for 5 more minutes and remove from heat so that the jicama remains crisp.

Serves 6 nicely with a salad.

WHITE BEAN CHILI

This chili, different in that it uses white Great Northern beans and chicken breasts, is a power house of flavor.

1 pound Great Northern or navy beans,
  cooked following recipe on page 121
1 12-ounce can of beer
2 cups diced onions
1 and 1/2 tablespoons minced garlic
1 cup diced red bell pepper
2 green chiles, charred, seeded, peeled
1 tablespoon oregano
1 tablespoon crushed cumin seeds
2 tablespoons ground red chile

PER SERVING:
481 calories
45 g protein
65 g carbohydrate
6 g fat
61 mg cholesterol
657 mg sodium

1 and 1/4 pounds skinned and boned chicken breast
1 pound tomatillos, husks removed
1 cup minced cilantro
1 tablespoon rice vinegar
1 teaspoon salt
1 14 and 1/2 ounce can fat-free chicken broth
1/2 cup reduced-fat sour cream
Cilantro leaves for garnish

While beans are cooking, prepare the other ingredients. Place beer in a large 4-quart pot and add onion, garlic, bell pepper, jalapeños, green chiles, oregano, and cumin. Simmer for 10 minutes until beer is reduced. This step takes the place of frying the vegetables.

Cut chicken into strips and then into dices. Add to the pot of simmering beer and vegetables. Sprinkle red chile over the top to color the chicken. Simmer for 15 minutes.

Place the tomatillos, cilantro, rice vinegar, and salt into a food processor and puree into a salsa. Stir the salsa into the chili pot, adding the chicken broth. Add the cooked white beans and continue to simmer for 20 more minutes.

Serve each bowl of White Bean Chili with a tablespoon of reduced-fat sour cream and a cilantro leaf. Serves 6.

CORN, THE SECOND FOOD OF THE TRINITY

Unlike California, where the native Indian and Spanish foods have disappeared from most tables, the real Southwest has prevailed particularly in New Mexico.

If soup is the soul of Mexican cuisine, corn is the heart of the Southwest, especially posole. Ingredients used for centuries such as the blue corn of the Pueblo Indians have survived and are thriving The magical bluish- gray corn not only provides more nourishment than the yellow but also has an earthier, richer flavor.

The special lime-treated corn, known as nixtamal, hominy, or posole is especially rich in calcium and is the ingredient ground into the masa (corn dough) used for corn tortillas, tamales, and the pupusas of Central America.

The whole kernels of posole, whose hulls have been removed, are used to make traditional posole stew. Posole is so important to feast days in both New Mexico and Mexico (spelled pozole there), it is often the focal point and most important food offered. With this book, I have carried on many inner battles between my taste buds and my desire to discover a more healthful style of eating; I worried about the endangered species—the rich, fatty native dishes. Stubbornly waging the battle, I did not cast away posole which can be considerably reduced in fats and still be wonderful.

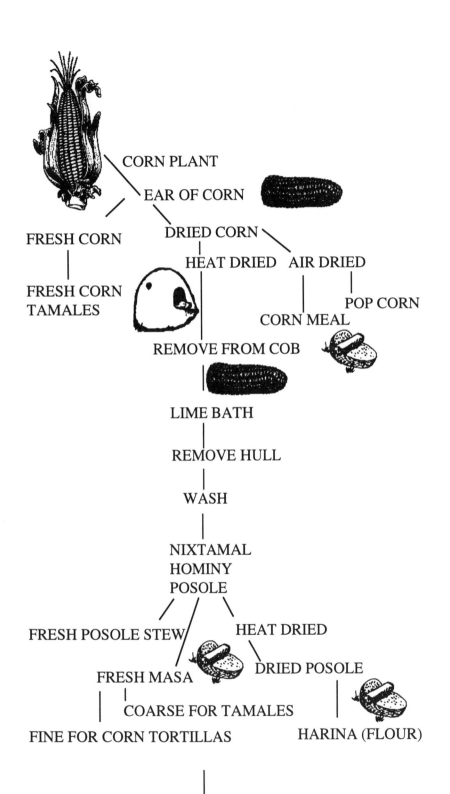

CORN PLANT

EAR OF CORN

FRESH CORN

DRIED CORN

FRESH CORN
TAMALES

HEAT DRIED   AIR DRIED

POP CORN

CORN MEAL

REMOVE FROM COB

LIME BATH

REMOVE HULL

WASH

NIXTAMAL
HOMINY
POSOLE

FRESH POSOLE STEW

HEAT DRIED

FRESH MASA

DRIED POSOLE

COARSE FOR TAMALES

FINE FOR CORN TORTILLAS

HARINA (FLOUR)

132 THE HOLY TRINITY

POSOLE

In the past I was always served posole at a fiesta or a saint's day and there was a mystique about it, daunting me to ever try making it without the help of an entire village. I put off testing this recipe which is a blend of 10 different recipes minus the traditional pig's head, pigs' feet, and pork shoulder. This recipe is far easier than most and it is my little triumph. It is so very good, it is one of the dishes I speak of when I say I could happily drown in the well of Mexican soups (and New Mexican stews).

1 pound of fresh or frozen nixtamal (hominy)
*   or 12 ounces of dried posole*
3 quarts of cold water
4 chicken legs with thighs attached, 2 and 1/2 pounds,
*   skin removed*
1 and 1/2 quarts fat-free homemade chicken broth
*   (see recipe, page 71 or 72)*
1 large onion, chopped
1 head of garlic, rinsed well and top sliced off
2 bay leaves
2 teaspoons oregano
1 teaspoon cracked black peppercorns
1/2 teaspoon salt
2 dried red New Mexican chile pods, stemmed and
*   seeded*
2 and 1/2 pounds pork tenderloins
2 teaspoons minced garlic
1 tablespoon ground red chile like New Mexican
*   Dixon*

PER SERVING:
521 calories
53 g protein
45 g carbohydrate
13 g fat
158 mg cholesterol
773 mg sodium

2 teaspoons olive oil
1 cup chopped onion
1 teaspoon minced garlic

Condiments to Serve with Posole:
2 cups of thinly sliced iceberg lettuce
1 bunch red radishes, thinly sliced
1/4 cup red ground chile
1 bunch green onions, sliced using half of the green tops
1/2 cup snipped cilantro
2 limes cut into small wedges

The day or night before you want to serve the posole, you must cook the nixtamal. First place the kernels in a large sieve and rinse under cold, running water for several minutes. Discard any discolored kernels. Place in a 5-quart pot and cover with 3 quarts of cold water. If you are using dried posole, simply rinse in a sieve. Cover with cold water and cook for approximately 2 hours or until tender. Do not add anything else, particularly salt, which will prevent the kernels from softening during the cooking. Cook the nixtamal on low heat for 2 to 3 hours until softened and the kernels burst or "flower." They will still have a certain firmness to the bite. Remove from heat when cooked. Place in a large bowl with some of the cooking liquid, cool down, and store covered in the refrigerator overnight.

The next day is posole day. Make sure you have removed all skin and fat from the chicken legs and

Note: Nixtamal, hominy and posole kernels are all the same thing—the skinned whole kernels of corn which have been processed in a water bath treated with unslaked lime and calcium carbonate. The dried posole is an excellent substitute for the fresh and can be ordered by mail (see Resources) and purchased in some Mexican stores.

Use fresh nixtamal (hominy) as it has a much more earthy and tasty flavor than canned hominy. Find a Mexican grocery store that sells masa and they will have fresh nixtamal.

thighs. You can leave them attached. My Mexican butcher thoughtfully leaves part of the backbone attached to the thigh. He believes this part adds great flavor. Place the chicken in a large pot containing the chicken broth, onion, head of garlic, bay leaves, oregano, crushed peppercorns, salt, and chile pods. Delete the salt if you are on a low-sodium diet. Simmer for about 45 minutes. Remove chicken to cool on a plate. This broth is heavenly and well worth our trouble.

Note: remove all skin and large pieces of fat from chicken; use lean pork loin; refrigerate posole so you may lift off any fat in broth.

Fix the pork loin. Preheat the oven to 400 degrees. Rub the pork with the garlic and ground chile. Roast for 45 minutes on a rack or broiler pan so that any fat may drip away. Usually a fattier cut is boiled in the broth. I think the roasting step adds flavor and removes most of the fat. Remove the roasted meat to a cutting board so it may cool.

Remove the cooled chicken from the bones and cut into small pieces. Cut the pork into 1-inch pieces. Place the chicken and the meat into the simmering broth. Drain the nixtamal of the watery liquid and add the kernels to the broth. Heat the oil in a pan and sauté the chopped onion and garlic for about 8 minutes until softened and golden. Add to the pot of posole. Simmer the posole for at least 45 more minutes once you have added everything to the pot.

You may chill the posole overnight. Using the above methods, you will not have much fat to remove from the top layer of the broth. The posole will become better in flavor and even freezes well.

When you are ready to serve, prepare all the condiments and pass them at the table for each person to add to their own bowl of posole. All that is needed are good corn tortillas and cold beer.

Serves 10 (or 8 hearty eaters) This recipe doubles and triples very well if you are serving a fiesta of posole eaters.

THE TAMALE PIE

Tamale pie always rises, like an old friend in a storm, along with the reminiscence of childhood in the fifties. My grandmother and mother made superb versions of this dish (recipes in my *California Rancho Cooking*) but I have revised and defatted this old standby and it is one of those homey dishes that still I crave once in awhile.

1 teaspoon olive oil
1 and 1/2 pounds ground turkey (7% fat)
1 cup chopped onion
2 teaspoons minced garlic
1 cup chopped bell pepper, red preferably
1/3 cup raisins
4 ounces tomato paste
1 cup water

2 teaspoons ground red chile (more if you need it hot)
1 can Mexicorn (11 ounces)
1/2 cup black olives, sliced
1 cup plus 2 tablespoons lowfat milk
1 teaspoon butter
1/3 cup cornmeal
1/4 teaspoon salt
1 whole egg, separated
1 egg white
2 tablespoons grated Parmesan cheese

First prepare the filling: sauté the crumbled ground turkey in the olive oil, adding the onion, garlic, and bell pepper after the turkey has lost its pink color, about 10 minutes.

Plump the raisins in hot water or place them in a small heatproof dish, sprinkle with 2 tablespoons water and zap in microwave on high power for 40 seconds. Add raisins to meat along with tomato paste, water, red chile, corn, and black olives. Simmer for 20 minutes.

Pour into a 1 and 1/2 quart baking dish. Set aside while you prepare the topping. Oven should be preheating to 375 degrees.

Heat milk, butter, and salt to a simmer. Stir in the cornmeal, blending well. Cook for about 2 minutes or until thickened. Stir the egg yolk and Parmesan into the warm cornmeal. Beat the 2 egg whites to soft peaks and fold into the cornmeal mush. Gently spread batter over the meat mixture in the baking dish.

Bake for 30 minutes or until the top is starting to color. This topping creates a golden corn layer akin to a corn pastry which you will love.

Serves 6 .

RANCHO COLACHE

PER SERVING:
95 calories
5 g protein
12 g carbohydrate
4 g fat
3 mg cholesterol
331 mg sodium

This squash stew, an old recipe from my grandmother, is one of the most flavorful ways to treat zucchini and goes well with tamale pie or enchiladas.

3 teaspoons olive oil
1 cup chopped onion
1 and 1/2 pounds zucchini, sliced thickly
4 green chiles (Anaheim), charred, peeled, seeded,
*   chopped*
1 teaspoon minced garlic
1 cup chopped red bell pepper
1 cup canned, crushed tomatoes
1/2 cup water
1/2 teaspoon salt
4 ears of corn (2 ounces each)
For topping, 1 ounce grated Asiago cheese

Heat oil and sauté onion until slightly softened, about 5 minutes. Push the onion to one side and sauté the zucchini slices until golden. Keep turning every couple of minutes. It is this browning step that adds flavor and was so important to my grandmother's way of doing it.

I have tried steaming all the vegetables together instead of sautéing and the flavor is simply not there. The bottom heat of the frying pan brings out greater flavor than steaming.

Next add the chile peppers, garlic, red pepper, tomatoes, water, and salt. Bury the ears of corn within all of the vegetables. Place a lid on top of the pan and simmer everything on low for about 15 minutes.

Sprinkle the Asiago cheese on top, simmer for a couple of minutes or just enough time for the cheese to melt.

6 servings.

CORN-BROWN RICE-LENTIL SALAD WITH JALAPEÑO VINAIGRETTE

For the simple days of the week, especially when I am busy, I keep this salad in the refrigerator for lovely sustenance.

1 and 1/2 cups cooked brown lentils
2 cups cooked brown basmati rice
1 can of corn niblets, 11 ounces
1 bunch chopped green onions, 1 cup
1 and 1/2 cups minced parsley
1/2 cup Jalapeño Vinaigrette (see page 141)
1 teaspoon ground red chile (Dixon)
Strips of red pepper or pimiento

PER SERVING:
193 calorie
8g protein
34 g carbohydrate
4 g fat
0 mg cholesterol
77 mg sodium

If you do not have on hand the cooked lentils, simply rinse 1 cup of dry lentils and place in a large pot with 2 quarts of cold water. Bring to a simmer and cook the lentils for 25 minutes. Do not overcook. Drain and rinse in cool water.

For the brown rice, I prefer my Japanese rice cooker; if you do not have a cooker simply bring to a simmer 2 and 1/2 cups water, 1 teaspoon low-sodium soy sauce, and add 1 cup of brown rice. Cook on low heat for 45 minutes. Do not lift the lid. Allow the rice to steam for 10 minutes with lid on after you have turned off the heat. Spread the rice out on a plate to cool before making the salad.

With a large fork, stir together the cooled rice, the lentils, onions, parsley, and corn. Sprinkle in the Jalapeño Vinaigrette and stir. I find it best to add 1/4 cup of the dressing now and then add more just before serving. Chill for at least 2 hours and then sprinkle with a little minced parsley and the ground chile. Some strips of red pepper also add the color that this brown salad needs.

Serves 6 generously.

JALAPEÑO VINAIGRETTE

PER SERVING:
41 calories
.14 g protein
1 g carbohydrate
4 g fat
0 mg cholesterol
93 mg sodium

3 tablespoon white wine vinegar
3 tablespoons lemon juice
1/4 cup water
3 tablespoon oil
1 teaspoon Dijon mustard
1/4 teaspoon ground cumin
1 teaspoon garlic, minced
1 tomato, skinned and seeded
1 pickled jalapeño chile
1/4 cup cilantro

In a food processor, place all of the above ingredients and blend. Tiny bits of chile and cilantro give the dressing character. This dressing is also good on taco salad and green salads.

Makes 1 and 1/4 cups

CORN ENCHILADAS

Surprise for people who think enchiladas are made of only cheese, beef, or chicken.

12 dried red New Mexican or California chiles
1 tablespoon oil
1 tablespoon flour
1/2 teaspoon ground cumin
1/2 teaspoon oregano
1/2 teaspoon sugar
1/2 teaspoon salt
1 cup reduced sodium chicken broth
1 teaspoon apple cider vinegar
Corn filling:
2 teaspoons canola oil
1 cup chopped onion
3 green Anaheim chiles, charred, skinned, seeded
1 red bell pepper, charred, skinned, seeded
2 cups corn kernels, fresh or frozen niblets
2 tablespoons lowfat sour cream (40 % less fat)
4 ounces reduced- fat Monterey Jack cheese
1 ounce of reduced fat Monterey Jack cheese for garnish
6 flour tortillas or 12 corn tortillas

Break apart the chiles, remove stems, and seeds. Rinse in cold water. Place in heatproof bowl and pour boiling water over them and steep chiles for 30 minutes. Place the soaked chiles and 1 cup water in a food processor or blender and puree. Use a rubber spatula to rub the puree through a strainer to remove chile skins.

Heat the tablespoon of oil and stir in the flour, cooking until golden, about 2 minutes. Slowly stir in the chile puree, blending out lumps with the spatula. Add the cumin, oregano, sugar, salt, vinegar, and chicken broth. Simmer the sauce for 20 minutes. Set aside while you prepare the filling.

Char the chiles and red pepper under a broiler or over a gas flame until they are blackened. Sauté the onion in the oil until softened and then stir in the chiles, peppers, and corn. Simmer over low heat for 10 minutes. Remove from heat and stir in the sour cream and grated cheese.

Heat the tortillas on a griddle to soften. If you want to further cut the calories, use corn instead of flour tortillas. Place 1 cup of chile sauce on a dinner plate and arrange corn filling near by. Dip the tortilla, both sides, in the chile sauce. Place 1/4 cup corn filling (for flour tortillas) toward one edge and roll up. Place enchilada in a wide rectangular, lightly oiled baking dish. Leave at least 1/2-inch between each enchilada so they do not stick to each other and become difficult to remove later.

Note: a wonderful, very Mexican addition to these enchiladas is to cook a diced red-skinned potato and carrot in an inch of water just until tender. Sprinkle with 2 tea-spoons white wine vinegar. Place a few of the vinegary cubes of carrot and potato over each enchilada just before serving.

When all the enchiladas are completed, sprinkle them with a little grated cheese and the reserved corn. Bake in a preheated 350 degree oven for 10 minutes.

Serves 6.

GREEN CORN TAMALES

I have searched for years for the perfect green corn tamale that is not laden with fat. It is quite easy to make a delicious tamale of fresh corn, lots of butter and shortening and cream. I made at least a dozen recipes before devising this one with a minimum of margarine and lowfat sour cream. These tamales are wonderfully succulent and I urge you to be creative with the filling such as using leftover chili.

2 pounds frozen corn niblets, thawed or kernels cut
  from 12 ears of corn= 6 cups kernels
1 and 1/2 tablespoons sugar
1/2 teaspoon salt
1/3 cup melted corn oil margarine
1/4 cup lowfat sour cream
3/4 cup cornmeal
1/2 teaspoon baking powder
Filling:
1 zucchini, ends removed, cut into sticks
1 potato, cooked and diced
4 ounces reduced-fat Jack or Cheddar cheese, cut into
  sticks
2 Anaheim green chiles, charred, skin and seeds
  removed, cut into strips
20 dried corn husks
24 pieces of 8-inch string
Tamale pot or large pot with steamer insert

Put the corn husks to soak in a sink filled with hot water. Soak for at least 1 hour.

Puree 3 cups of the corn kernels in a food processor until fairly smooth. Dump into a large bowl. Add the next 3 cups of corn to the food processor and puree also. Next add the melted margarine, sour cream, sugar, and salt. Blend together briefly and then add to the bowl. Stir in the cornmeal and the baking powder.

Place a long length of heavy paper towel on the counter and place the husks on one end to drain. Have ready the corn batter, the filling, the lengths of string, and the tamale pot.

Place an opened corn husk in front of you. Spread 1/3 cup of corn batter in a 4" x 4" square on the husk, closer to one edge of the husk and leaving the bottom and top of the husk bare so it may be tied. Place a stick of zucchini, a cube of potato, a strip of green chile and a stick of cheese on top of the corn batter. Sometimes I sprinkle these with ground red chile for more color. Fold over the sides of the corn husks and use a piece of string to tie off each end.

Place 4 or 5 opened corn husks on top of the steamer basket in the pot. You should have already added 2 inches of water to the pot. Lay each completed tamale on top of the bed of husks. You do not have to stand these tamales on their ends. Finish the rest of the tamales. You should have at least 12. If you make them bigger, you might end up with just 9 or 10 fat tamales.

Bring pot to a boil and then lower the heat; steam the tamales on low heat for 35 minutes. Remove the tamales from the pot immediately.

Serves only 6 people who can easily eat 2 each.

PAN DE MAÍZ

PER SERVING:
254 calories
19 g protein
19 g carbohydrate
12 g fat
50 mg cholesterol
230 mg sodium

On my family's land grant rancho in California, they served a corn and chicken dish called Chileña Pie which was a feast dish for special occasions. I simplified it so I didn't need a cast of hundreds to prepare it (when my grandmother made it she had a roomful of dedicated cooks to help her). Pan de Maíz is to be enjoyed during the week for a simple meal.

3 cups (12 ounces) light and dark chicken meat (removed from 1 and 1/2 pound roasted chicken)
16 ounce package frozen corn niblets, thawed
1/4 cup melted margarine
2 teaspoons sugar
1/4 teaspoon salt
1 tablespoon cornmeal
1/2 teaspoon sugar

Cut the chicken into large 2-inch pieces. Sometimes when I am in a hurry I buy a rotisserie-roasted chicken from the supermarket. As soon as you get the warm chicken home, pull off the skin and remove chicken from the bones so the fat does not have a chance to penetrate the meat.

Use a food processor or blender to puree the corn until smooth. Add the margarine, sugar, and salt. Blend quickly.

Lightly oil a deep 9 by 13-inch baking dish. Spread a thin layer of the pureed corn on the bottom. Place a middle layer of chicken, using the total amount. Spread the rest of the pureed corn on top. Sprinkle the top with the cornmeal and sugar.

Bake in a preheated 350 degree oven for 40 minutes or until the corn is golden around the edges.

A fruit salad is a perfect accompaniment.

Serves 6.

CHICKEN CHILI

One cold winter afternoon I enjoyed a bowl of delicious chicken chili at our local health food store, The Whole Wheatery. Their chili served as my inspiration and it was with concoctions such as this that I became fairly convinced one can dine well without fatty ingredients. Each bowl of Chicken Chili has only 6 grams of fat.

PER SERVING:
234 calories
24 g protein
22 g carbohydrate
6 g fat
62 mg cholesterol
523 mg sodium

3 and 1/4 pound chicken, skin removed
1 quart water
1 can beer (12 ounces)
1 cup chopped onion
1 cup of chopped celery, including leaves
1 tablespoon oregano
1 and 1/2 teaspoons ground cumin
1 tablespoon minced garlic
1 can ready-cut tomatoes, 28 ounces
1 can Rotel tomatoes (10 ounces)
1/4 cup mild or hot ground red chile
1 cup cooked beans (anasazi or pinto)
Cooked chicken from above
1 cup chicken broth from cooking chicken
1 cup frozen corn niblets
3/4 cup sliced black olives

I pressure-cook my chicken in 1 quart of water for 30 minutes. You can simmer the chicken for 45 minutes in a regular 5-quart pot. In the pressure cooker, the chicken remains juicy and the resulting broth is much better.

While the chicken is cooking, add the beer to a 5-quart pot along with the celery, onion, garlic, oregano, cumin, and simmer until almost all of the beer is reduced to half its original amount. This step takes the place of sautéing in oil.

While the onion mixture is cooking in the beer, roughly puree the tomatoes. If Rotel tomatoes are unavailable, substitute stewed tomatoes in the same amount. Add the tomato puree to the onions and beer. Stir in the ground chile and the cooked beans. Simmer for 30 minutes partially covered

Cool the chicken (you should have about 32 ounces of chicken) on a plate and then remove meat from the bones. Chop in small pieces. Stir the chicken into the chili mixture. Simmer for another 20 minutes, adding the cup of reserved broth. Add the corn (during all the cooking I remove the corn niblets from the freezer so they may thaw) and the olives. Simmer for 15 minutes longer.

Serves 8.

BLUE CORN BANANA MUFFINS

Through two cookbooks I have searched far and wide for the most perfect blue corn muffin and the favorite has finally emerged from my testing. It had to be light and sweet enough to balance the earthiness of the blue corn. The small amount of banana, the magic ingredient, gives a lovely moistness and sweetness. You can freeze the rest of the banana for breakfast drinks or pancakes or just stand there and eat it while the muffins are baking.

1 cup of finely ground blue corn flour
1/2 cup whole wheat pastry flour
1/2 cup unbleached all-purpose flour
2 teaspoons baking powder
1/2 teaspoon baking soda
1 tablespoon sugar
1/4 cup melted corn oil margarine
2 tablespoons honey
2 tablespoons mashed banana
2 egg whites
1/2 cup nonfat yogurt
1/2 cup lowfat milk (2%)

Preheat oven to 400 degrees and spray a 12-cup muffin tin with Baker's Joy. Over a large bowl, sift together the blue corn flour (often referred to as blue corn atole in the Southwest), the whole wheat, the all-purpose flour, baking powder, baking soda, and sugar.

Melt the margarine. Stir in the honey.

In a small bowl, beat together the nonfat yogurt and milk until well-blended and then whisk in the egg whites. Next whisk in the mashed bananas so there are not any large lumps.

PER SERVING:
135 calories
3 g protein
21 g carbohydrate
4 g fat
1 mg cholesterol
172 mg sodium

Pour the yogurt mixture over the dry flour mixture in the bowl and over this pour the melted margarine-honey mixture. Mix just until blended and there are no dry spots. Do not over mix.

Spoon the batter into the 12 muffin cups and bake for about 14 to 15 minutes. The muffins will be a little golden around the edges when they are done. If you are serving these for a party, it is fun to tear off 2-inch strips of dry corn husk and soak in hot water for 10 minutes to soften. Fit the husk strips into each muffin cup. Spray with Baker's Joy and spoon the batter over the husk. This is an attractive Southwestern way to bake the muffins.

Makes 12 medium muffins.

PART IV CHILES,
THE APEX OF THE TRINITY

If corn is the foundation of Southwestern foods then chiles are the key to unlocking the door of authentic native cooking. In New Mexico as in Mexico, many of the most popular dishes revolve around chiles. A chile is not just a chile but a specific type, carrying with it a whole gamut of traits which dictate its destination - from mole to salsa.

Salsamania has spread from west to east. With general interest heightened, more cooks are aware that chiles can go beyond salsa. While the commercial growers in southern New Mexico try to keep pace with the escalating appetite for chiles by growing milder strains, independent farmers on small plots nurse their native plants, often from seeds kept in families for generations.

Perhaps it is the dry climate and the particular mounds of dirt where they are grown which bequeaths to them a richer flavor but I cannot live without the Chimayo and Dixon chiles of northern New Mexico. When I am down to 1 pound of Dixon chile powder, I call up for more.

When you cook with flavorful, full-bodied chiles as opposed to the red dust often sold as chile powder, you need less salt in your cooking especially when the chile is combined with an abundance of garlic and other spices.

GREEN CHILE STEW

PER SERVING:
271 calories
27 g protein
27 g carbohydrate
6 g fat
74 mg cholesterol
172 mg sodium

Of all the unusual and exotic dishes that come out of my kitchen, this stew is my sons' favorite. They love the chunks of browned meat, carrots, and potatoes—all identifiable foods where their mother doesn't appear to have hidden anything suspicious. This is one of the most widely eaten stews in the Southwest.

1 and 1/2 pounds pork tenderloin
2 teaspoons ground red chile
2 teaspoons ground cumin
1 tablespoon oregano
2 teaspoons oil
1 cup chopped onion
1 tablespoon minced garlic
3 cups homemade chicken stock or reduced sodium
    chicken broth
1 bay leaf
2 jalapeño chiles, seeded and minced
1/2 pound Anaheim green chiles (about 4), charred,
    peeled, seeded, and chopped
1 pound red-skinned potatoes, cut in half
1 bunch carrots, about 2 cups cut into 3" pieces

Cut the meat into 3-inch chunks and rub with the chile, cumin, and oregano. Heat the oil in a heavy 5-quart pot (I use a Le Cruset enameled cast-iron pot) and brown the meat chunks 3 batches at a time, removing as it browns. When all the meat is ready, sauté the onion until softened. Next stir in the garlic, the stock, and the bay leaf. Put all of the browned meat back into the pot. Simmer for 30 minutes.

While the meat is simmering, prepare the chiles by charring and removing the skins and seeds. Chop the chiles and stir into the meat along with the chopped jalapeños.

Prepare the vegetables and add them to the pot. Simmer until they are tender, 20 to 25 minutes. Serve meat and vegetables with some of the chile broth in wide soup bowls. Serve blue corn muffins or corn bread as an accompaniment.

6 servings

GREEN CHILE

ROASTING TO REMOVE SKIN

RED CHILE (RIPE)

FREEZE

HEAT DRIED

AIR DRIED (RISTRA)

GREEN CHILE STEW

WHOLE CHILES

CHILE RELLENOS

GROUND CHILE

GROUND CHILE MIXED WITH
SPICES=CHILE POWDER

154 THE HOLY TRINITY

TURKEY BREAST GREEN CHILE STEW

Here is another version of the traditional green chile stew.

2 and 1/2 pounds boned turkey breast, skin removed
2 teaspoons olive oil
1 cup chopped onion
2 teaspoons minced garlic
6 green Anaheim chiles, charred, skins and seeds
    removed or 2 cans green chiles (7 ounces each)
2 teaspoons oregano
1 bay leaf
1/4 teaspoon cinnamon
3 teaspoons dried ground green chile (see Resources)
4 cups reduced sodium chicken broth or homemade
    chicken broth
2 sweet potatoes, peeled, cut into chunks
1 tablespoons flour
1/4 cup light sour cream (40% fat)
1/2 avocado, 8 slices for garnish

Cut turkey into large 2-inch chunks and dry well with a paper towel. Heat the oil and brown the turkey in 3 batches, removing pieces from pan as they brown. Next add the onion to the pan and sauté until softened. Stir in the garlic. Chop the chiles and add to pan along with the spices and chicken broth. The dried green chile adds great flavor but the stew will still be good without it. Simmer the turkey for 20 minutes.

PER SERVING:
219 calories
29 g protein
14 g carbohydrate
5 g fat
70 mg cholesterol
115 mg sodium

Add the sweet potato chunks and simmer for 20 minutes longer. Stir the flour into the sour cream and blend this mixture into the simmering broth. Gently cook for 2 minutes and remove from heat.

8 servings.

SANTA FE STROGANOFF

Beef eaters rejoice, I have not forgotten your existence. Flank steak, when marinated and cut on the cross-grain, is quite tender and very flavorful. Best of all, it is a leaner cut.

PER SERVING:
316 calories
26 g protein
9 g carbohydrate
17 g fat
66 mg cholesterol
333 mg sodium

1 flank steak, 1 and 1/2 pounds
2 teaspoons olive oil
1/4 cup red wine vinegar
1 teaspoon low sodium soy sauce (7.6 % sodium)
2 teaspoons Worcestershire sauce
1 teaspoon oregano
1 teaspoon black pepper
1 teaspoon minced garlic
4 green chiles, charred, skins and seeds removed,
*   chopped or use canned chiles*
1 can 14 and 1/2 ounce can fat-free chicken broth or
*   homemade broth, see page 71*
1 teaspoon olive oil
1 pound button mushrooms
1/2 cup light sour cream (40% less fat)
1/4 cup cilantro, snipped with scissors
2 teaspoons ground red chile

Slice the flank steak across the grain into 1/2-inch slices and then cut the slices in half, into strips. Make a marinade of the olive oil, vinegar, soy sauce, Worcestershire sauce, oregano, black pepper, and garlic. Rub this into the meat strips and marinate for at least a couple of hours.

In a separate skillet, simmer the chopped green chiles and chicken broth for 15 minutes.

After the meat has marinated spray a sauté pan with Pam and quickly sear the meat strips in 3 batches. Remove each batch to the skillet containing the chiles. Simmer all of the browned meat in the chile-broth for 15 minutes.

Wash the mushrooms quickly under running water. Wipe clean with a soft paper towel and slice. Meanwhile, add 1 teaspoon of olive oil to the sauté pan you used for the meat. Sauté the mushrooms for 2 minutes. Add to the meat during the last 5 minutes of simmering. Stir in the sour cream and half of the cilantro, reserving the rest for garnish. Do not simmer the sour cream too long or it will curdle. Place the Stroganoff in a serving dish and sprinkle with minced cilantro and a couple of teaspoons of ground red chile. This dish is quite good when served over noodles, especially red pepper or chile noodles.

6 servings

VEGETABLE BURRITOS WITH KILLER RED SAUCE

PER SERVING:
279 calories
13 g protein
34 g carbohydrate
10 g fat
29 mg cholesterol
384 mg sodium

A vegetable burrito should be covered with the same kind of sauce you would put over a delightfully greasy carnita (fried pork bits) burrito. If you are going to win over an occasional carnivore, you will not do it using kid gloves. Leave them, your eaters that is, breathless and they won't care what's inside the burrito.

2 teaspoons olive oil
1 cup red onion, chopped
1 and 1/2 cup mixed frozen vegetables
1/4 cup roasted red bell peppers from jar
1 cup diced zucchini
1/2 cup Jacquie's Everyday Salsa, see page 172 or
*   good store-bought salsa*
8 ounces of grated partially- skim mozzarella cheese
6 flour tortillas (10-inch)
Killer Red Sauce, recipe below

Heat the olive oil in a nonstick skillet and sauté the onion on very low heat for 15 to 20 minutes or until soft and caramelized. This onion marmalade will add considerable flavor to any steamed vegetables.

Steam together the mixed frozen vegetables, the red peppers, and the diced zucchini for about 10 minutes until just tender. Use a saucepan with a steamer basket if possible. The last minute of steaming, sprinkle the mozzarella cheese over the top of the vegetables. Watch carefully as the cheese will melt in less than a minute and you do not want it to drip down into the steaming water!

Place the steamed vegetables and cheese into a bowl and stir in the salsa and sautéed onions.

Warm each flour tortilla just enough on a griddle so you may fold it into the burrito without cracking. Place a scant 1/2 cup of vegetable-salsa filling down the middle of the tortilla. Fold over each end of burrito and then fold one side to the center over the filling and then the other side. Place on a plate and cover with warmed Killer Red Sauce or briefly heat the folded burrito on the hot griddle and serve it naked. Just douse it with more salsa.

KILLER RED SAUCE

Dried red chiles can sometimes be too potent unless you were born in New Mexico or you are one of those converts more avid than the natives.

By simmering the dried chiles with tomato, onion, and garlic the chiles are sweetened and I think their flavor is boosted. Without a doubt, this has become one of my favorite red sauces. As a bonus, this chile sauce isn't thickened with the fat and flour roux that is traditional.

12 dried red chiles (New Mexican, California, ancho),
*   about 3 ounces*
4 cups water
1 /2 cup chopped onion

PER SERVING:
36 calories
1 g protein
7 g carbohydrate
1 g fat
0 mg cholesterol
59 mg sodium

3 cloves whole, unskinned garlic
1 and 1/2 cups chopped, unskinned tomatoes (about 8
*   ounces)*
1/4 teaspoon salt
1/2 teaspoon sugar

Place the dried chiles on a baking sheet and toast in a preheated 250 degree oven for 6 minutes. Do not brown them or the chiles will become bitter. Remove and place in a sink filled with cold water. Rinse the chiles off. Remove stems and seeds.

In 2-quart pot, simmer chiles, tomatoes, onion, garlic, salt and sugar in water for 30 minutes. Cook with the lid on and every 5 minutes push the chiles back down into the liquid. The chiles will absorb a lot of the liquid.

Puree everything in a food processor (in 2 batches) and push through a wire strainer to remove skins.

Simmer the sauce in a skillet for at least 5 minutes to concentrate flavors.

Makes approximately 2 and 1/2 cups chile sauce or 1/4 cup servings for 10 enchiladas or burritos. Freezes beautifully.

CHICKEN COLORADO

Chile colorado is one of my husband's favorite Mexican dishes but it is usually made with a cut of meat that is very fatty. This is one of those instances when having a refrigerator of sauces from my numerous tests has come in handy. I combined chunks of poached chicken with the Killer Red Sauce above and came up with Chicken Colorado, which makes great burritos especially if you have some beans on hand.

3 cups light and dark chicken meat, removed from 1
    and 1/2 pound poached chicken
2 and 1/2 cups Killer Red Sauce (see page 159)
1 teaspoon toasted cumin seeds, ground

To poach a chicken, use the directions for Friendly Chicken Broth on page 72 but reduce 20 minutes from the cooking time, removing the chicken early even if you are using a pressure cooker.

Pull the cooked chicken from the bones and cut into large 2 or 3-inch chunks. Place in a 3-quart pot with the Killer Red Sauce and cumin. Simmer on low for 30 minutes with lid partially on. Stir frequently as chile sauce tends to stick and burn. If sauce becomes too thick, add 1/2 cup poaching liquid from chicken or plain water.

4 servings or 6 burritos using 10-inch flour tortillas.

PER SERVING:
252 calories
28 g protein
17 g carbohydrate
10 g fat
76 mg cholesterol
220 mg sodium

ENCHILADAS OF THE JARDÍN

PER SERVING:
150 calories
6 g protein
26 g carbohydrate
4 g fat
5 mg cholesterol
155 mg sodium

The first year that I lived in San Miguel de Allende, Mexico I often strolled the jardín at dusk. The cooking women, in front of their smoky braziers, were like figures in the pattern of an old tapestry.

I often lingered to watch each woman's cooking style, listening to their banter and watching their deft hands create instant enchiladas as they wrapped up crumbled queso ranchero and chopped raw onions in the fresh tortillas.

The enchiladas, doused with red chile sauce, were hot in a minute and rolled out onto a terra cotta plate. If I remained too long, captivated by the skillets, the women knew I could not resist their offerings.

Sometimes when we are barbecuing, I put a heavy cast-iron skillet at one end of the grill and cook these enchiladas. Somehow they must be imbued with mesquite smoke to taste exactly right.

2 and 1/2 cups Killer Red Sauce. See recipe on page 159.
12 corn tortillas
1 cup chopped onion, soaked in cold water
3/4 cup crumbled farmer's cheese (or goat's cheese)
3 carrots, diced
2 red-skinned potatoes, diced
1 bay leaf
1 tablespoon cider vinegar
Pink Pickled Onions, see recipe, page 41

Warm 1 and 1/2 cups of the Killer Red Sauce in a heavy 12-inch skillet, preferably cast-iron. Drain the chopped onions and pat dry.

Spray a nonstick skillet with oil and heat one tortilla at a time. When the tortilla is warm and pliable, dip in the red sauce and place on a flat plate. Sprinkle 1 tablespoon cheese and a teaspoon of onion down the middle. Roll up into a tube or enchilada.

Simmer the carrots and potatoes in water to cover with the bay leaf for about 12 minutes or just until tender. Remove to a plate and sprinkle with the vinegar while still warm. Add the Pink Pickled Onions to the plate.

Add 1/2 cup red sauce to the skillet and heat 6 enchiladas at a time. This takes just a minute. Place 2 enchiladas on each plate and sprinkle with some of the diced carrots and potatoes and a couple of rings of Pink Pickled Onions.

12 enchiladas for 6 people.

EGGPLANT ENCHILADAS

PER SERVING:
156 calories
7 g protein
22 g carbohydrate
5 g fat
7 mg cholesterol
176 mg sodium

I am resurrecting these enchiladas from my *California Rancho* cookbook because they are so good. But I have learned to lessen the amount of olive oil and cheese! People actually mistake the pieces of eggplant for meat.

3 teaspoons olive oil
1 and 1/2 cups chopped onion
2 cups of peeled, diced eggplant
3 teaspoons oregano
1 cup grated reduced fat Cheddar cheese
12 corn tortillas
2 and 1/2 cups Killer Red Sauce, see page 159
Pam for spraying sauté pan
1/2 cup lowfat, plain yogurt
1/4 cup minced green onions

Heat the olive oil in a nonstick skillet and sauté the onions until they are very soft, about 20 minutes.

Meanwhile, place the eggplant cubes in a vegetable steamer. Steam for 8 minutes. Blot off excess moisture with paper towels and add to the skillet containing the sautéed onions. Cook the onions and eggplant together for about 10 minutes, adding the oregano.

Spray a nonstick skillet with Pam and heat each corn tortilla just enough to soften. Dip both sides of the tortilla in Killer Red Sauce. Lay the dipped tortilla on a flat diner plate. Down the middle place a couple of tablespoons of eggplant-onion mixture and a tablespoon of grated cheese. Fold over sides.

Place the enchiladas in a long, greased baking dish Bake in a preheated 350 degree oven for 15 minutes or until cheese is melted. Do not bake too long or you will end up with a casserole.

Stir the minced green onions into the yogurt and use for garnish over each enchilada.

Makes 12 enchiladas for 6 people

ENCHILADAS VERDES

These enchiladas are done with my new great discovery, Tomatillo Salsa cooked in the microwave. In Mexico they often add 2 cups of crema doble, like creme fraiche, to the tops of the enchiladas and then they become Enchiladas Suizas (Swiss).

PER SERVING:
201 calories
15 g protein
18 g carbohydrate
8 g fat
35 mg cholesterol
174 mg sodium

1 and 3/4 pound poached or roasted chicken, skin
    removed with 12 ounces of light and dark meat
2 teaspoons canola oil
1 cup chopped onion
1/2 cup diced green chiles, fresh or canned
2 teaspoons oil for frying tortillas, divided
12 corn tortillas
3 cups Tomatillo Salsa, see page 167
1/2 cup light sour cream (40% less fat)
3 tablespoons lowfat milk (2% fat)
1 tablespoon minced green onion
1 cup grated reduced-fat Monterey Jack cheese

To poach a chicken, use the directions on page 72 but subtract 20 minutes from the cooking time and remove the chicken early even if you are using a pressure cooker. If you are in a great hurry, you can buy a rotisserie-roasted chicken from the supermarket. Don't chill it unless you remove the fatty skin first.

Remove the cooked chicken from the bones. Heat the oil in a sauté pan and cook the onions over low heat until softened. Add the green chiles and cook together for about 5 more minutes. Fresh green chiles that have been charred and peeled have the most flavor but use canned chiles if you are in a hurry. Set aside and stir in chicken.

Heat 1 teaspoon of oil in a nonstick 10-inch skillet. Warm each tortilla in the skillet until it is soft and pliable. Dip both sides of the tortilla into the Tomatillo Salsa (which will only lightly coat it) and lay it out on a flat dinner plate. Place about 2 tablespoons of the chicken-chile filling in each tortilla. Roll up and place in an oiled baking dish. You will need 2 baking dishes for 12 enchiladas or 1 jelly-roll pan. Drizzle more salsa on tops of enchiladas and sprinkle with grated cheese. Bake in a preheated 350 degree oven for 15 minutes. During the last 5 minutes of baking, combine the sour cream, milk, and green onions. Drizzle over the tops of the enchiladas.

You have to be careful about overbaking enchiladas made out of tortillas that have not been heavily fried as they tend to fall apart more if you bake them too long. Pour more heated salsa over the enchiladas just before serving.

Makes 12 enchiladas for 6 people.

FAST TOMATILLO SALSA

Cooking the tomatillos quickly in the microwave oven helps retain a sweeter and brighter flavor.

1 and 1/2 pounds tomatillos
1/2 cup chopped onion
4 jalapeño chiles, stems and some seeds removed
3 cloves garlic, in pieces
1/2 cup cilantro
1 teaspoon vinegar
1/4 teaspoon salt
1/2 teaspoon sugar

Soak tomatillos in a sink full of warm water to soften the dry husks. After 2 minutes of soaking, peel off the husks. Place tomatillos on a flat dinner plate and microwave on high power for 225 seconds (for a 600 watt oven).

Place the tomatillos in a food processor and chop roughly; add the rest of the ingredients and puree. I always leave some of the veins and seeds in the chiles because tomatillos have a mysterious way of obliterating hot chiles. If you like really hot salsa, you may have to add at least 1 more chile to those required in the recipe. Maybe you'll want to add 2 more chiles!

Makes 1 quart of salsa or 16 servings.

PER SERVING:
15 calories
.7 g protein
3 g carbohydrate
.2 g fat
0 mg cholesterol
34 mg sodium

Note: add 1 tablespoon pureed chipotle en adobo for spicier salsa.

SPICY TURKEY TENDERLOINS WITH RED PEPPER SAUCE

PER SERVING:
191 calories
28 g protein
6 g carbohydrate
6 g fat
71 mg cholesterol
210 mg sodium

Cooking turkey tenderloins with the beer method retains the juiciness of the meat. Sometimes I serve these with both the Fast Tomatillo Salsa and the Red Pepper Sauce. Rice or noodles are a perfect accompaniment.

2 turkey tenderloins, 12 ounces each
1 teaspoon granulated garlic
1 teaspoon oregano
2 teaspoons ground red chile
1/4 teaspoon salt
1 teaspoon dried thyme leaves
2 teaspoons olive oil for sautéing turkey
1 cup beer
2 red bell peppers
2 teaspoons oil for sautéing garlic and onions
2 cloves garlic, minced through press
1/4 cup chopped onion
1 tablespoon tomato paste
1 teaspoon dried thyme leaves
1/2 cup dry white wine
1 cup reduced-sodium chicken broth
1 tablespoon lowfat sour cream (40% less fat)
1/4 cup parsley, minced

Blend the granulated garlic, oregano,chile,salt, and thyme together and rub over the tenderloins. Let them marinate at room temperature while you prepare the Red Pepper Sauce.

Char the red peppers over a gas flame or under a broiler until they are completely blistered and blackened. Steam them for 10 minutes in a plastic bag and then scrape the skins off with a small knife and cut out the stems and cores. Cut the peppers into small pieces.

Sauté the garlic and onion in the oil for 5 minutes and then add the red peppers and sauté for a couple of minutes. Next add the tomato paste, the thyme, the wine, and the chicken stock. Simmer for 10 minutes, until reduced by half. Place everything in a food processor and puree. Remove and stir in the sour cream. Set aside while you cook the turkey tenderloins.

Heat the oil in a nonstick skillet that has a tight-fitting lid. Add both of the tenderloins and sauté about a minute on each side or just enough to lightly brown. Add the cup of beer and clamp on the lid. Simmer the tenderloins for a total of 20 minutes. Every 5 minutes turn them and push around in the beer sauce. This is also a great way to cook strips of boned chicken breast for fast fajitas.

Serve slices of the turkey with warm Red Pepper Sauce, sprinkled with minced parsley.

6 servings

CHICKEN RÁPIDO

Everyone adores this simple recipe and best of all it's easy on the cook. All you need is a tossed salad.

1 cup finely ground baked (no oil) tortilla chips
1 cup finely ground flaked whole wheat cereal (Nutri-grain)
1 package taco seasoning (1 and 1/4 ounces)
2 egg whites
24 ounces of boned, skinned chicken breasts, cut into strips
1 and 1/2 tablespoons melted margarine

Grind the tortilla chips, cereal, and taco seasoning together in a food processor. Place the crumbs on a flat dinner plate.

Beat the egg whites with a fork until they are foamy.

Dip the chicken strips into the egg whites and then into the crumbs.

Place on a jelly roll pan sprayed with Pam. After all of the chicken strips are coated, drizzle with the margarine. Bake in a preheated 350 degree oven for about 18 minutes until chicken strips are golden and crispy.

6 servings.

PER SERVING:
2 chicken strips
135 calories
15 g protein
12 g carbohydrate
2 g fat
33 mg cholesterol
360 mg sodium

Note:you can make your own taco seasoning by combining 1 tablespoon ground red chile, 1/2 teaspoon cumin, 1 teaspoon oregano, and 1/2 teaspoon salt.

SOFT TACOS WITH SALSAS

Soft tacos are the only tacos I remember in Mexico and now in Southern California there are a number of joints that grill marinated chicken and beef, fold them into warm corn tortillas, and allow you to find your way through a salsa bar. But now you can make them at home.

24 ounces of skinned, boned chicken breast
2 tablespoons lemon juice
2 teaspoons olive oil
1 teaspoon minced garlic
1/2 teaspoon salt
1/2 teaspoon black pepper
1/4 cup chopped onion
1/4 cup minced cilantro
12 corn tortillas

Marinate the chicken breast meat in lemon juice, olive oil, garlic, salt, and black pepper.

Broil or grill about 5 minutes per side. Place the grilled chicken on a chopping board and chop into small pieces. Mix up the chicken with the onion and cilantro.

Warm tortillas on a griddle or in a microwave just until soft and warm.

Place chicken filling in the middle of each tortilla and let each person add his choice of salsa: Fast Tomatillo Salsa, page 167. Recipes for Hacked-up Salsa and Jacquie's Everyday Salsa are given below.

Makes 12 soft tacos for 6 people although I've known some men who can eat 4.

PER SERVING:
138 calories
15 g protein
13 g carbohydrate
2 g fat
33 mg cholesterol
182 mg sodium

HACKED-UP SALSA

PER SERVING:
72 calories
1 g protein
7 g carbohydrate
5 g fat
0 mg cholesterol
100 mg sodium

3 medium tomatoes, diced
1/2 cup diced white onion
1 jalapeño chile, minced (include seeds in this salsa)
1 avocado, skinned, seed removed, diced
3 teaspoons lime juice
1/4 teaspoon salt
1 tablespoon cilantro

Mix everything together and serve immediately. If you like it hot add another chile.

3 cups salsa for 6 servings because everyone eats it like salad.

JACQUIE'S EVERYDAY SALSA

PER SERVING:
16 calories
.6 g protein
3 g carbohydrate
.1 g fat
0 mg cholesterol
75 mg sodium

There is always a big jar of this medium-hot salsa in my refrigerator and I stir it into anything that needs a lift.

4 ounces tomatillos
2 pounds tomatoes
1 cup chopped onions
1/2 cup chopped green onions
1 tablespoon minced garlic
1/2 cup green chiles from can (about 2 chiles)
1/2 cup jalapeño chiles, some seeds removed
2 teaspoons ground red chile
1/2 teaspoon ground cumin
1/2 teaspoon salt
1/2 cup minced cilantro
3 tablespoons white wine vinegar

Soak the tomatillos in warm water and remove the dry husks. Dip the tomatoes in boiling water for 30 seconds to loosen the skins or hold over a gas flame and char. Remove the skins and squeeze out seeds.

Roughly puree everything in food processor.

Simmer salsa in an open 2-quart saucepan for 5 minutes to blend favors and help preserve the salsa. Salsa keeps well. If you want the salsa even hotter, just dice 2 more chiles, including the veins and seeds.

Makes 5 and 1/2 cups

INSIDE-OUT QUESADILLA WITH SMOKED FIRE

Quesadillas are survival food. Instead of folding the tortilla over grated cheese, as is usually done, these quesadillas are painted with a smoldering salsa first. When you are in a hurry and think you are starving hungry, this is what you need. These also give you a salsa fix.

2 flour tortillas (8-inch)
4 tablespoons Smoked Fire (page 175)
4 tablespoons grated reduced-fat Monterey Jack cheese (1/3 less fat)

PER SERVING:
159 calories
7 g protein
25 g carbohydrate
3 g fat
10 mg cholesterol
355 mg sodium

Fold over each flour tortilla and paint the top half with 2 tablespoons of Smoked Fire each. Sprinkle 2 tablespoons cheese over each folded half.

Broil in toaster oven or under broiler for about 1 and 1/2 minutes or until cheese is bubbly and tortilla is crisp around the edges.

Makes 2 servings.

SMOKED FIRE

This salsa is wonderfully complex and is likely to cause an addiction in anyone who loves extra hot food.

1 can plum tomatoes (28 ounces), drained
4 chipotle chiles en adobo from can
4 cloves garlic

Place everything in a food processor and puree. This salsa will keep for a couple of weeks in the refrigerator.

14 servings

PER SERVING:
14 calories
.6 g protein
3 g carbohydrate
.1 g fat
0 mg cholesterol
155 mg sodium

LICUADOS

CHAPTER VII

LICUADOS AND AQUAS FRESAS OF MEXICO

exicans, except for their national sweet tooth have a healthy diet high in carbohydrates, fruits, and vegetables. Especially healthy is their love of the fruit drinks called licuados, made either with strained fruit juice and sugar or pureed whole fruits.

At the very heart of the old San Miguel market, raised up on a platform, was the licuado lady with her array of tropical fruits and several blenders. After telling her the blend of fruits you wanted, she pureed them straight up or at your request added some milk. After a night of sipping vino tinto in one of the cafes, our parched mouths paid many early morning visits to the licuado lady.

SAN MIGUEL MARKET LICUADO

PER SERVING:
166 calories
2 g protein
40 g carbohydrate
.7 g fat
0 mg cholesterol
6 mg sodium

This licuado is particularly good with a Mexican or New Mexican breakfast focused on chiles. It is loaded with beta carotene and a beautiful sunny orange color which looks best in clear glasses. The recipe doubles easily.

1/2 cup diced fresh mango
1/2 cup diced fresh pineapple
1/2 cup sliced banana
1 cup fresh orange juice
1/2 papaya nectar blend (papaya puree, white grape
*   juice, and pineapple juice)*

Puree everything in a blender.

2 servings.

FRUIT RAINBOW LICUADO

PER SERVING:
126 calories
2 g protein
29 g carbohydrate
.6 g fat
0 mg cholesterol
6 mg sodium

In East Los Angeles licuados are a staple in many of the small family restaurants owned by Mexicans, Cubans, and Salvadorans. The Rainbow is one of the most popular in the Los Burritos licuado bar. Drink this in a beautiful glass and pretend you're at a health spa.

8 ounces fresh orange juice
1/2 cup papaya nectar delight (blend of white grape
*   juice, pineapple juice and papaya puree)*
1/2 cup boysenberries fresh or frozen

1/2 cup fresh strawberries
1/2 cup diced watermelon

Puree everything in a blender.

2 servings (approximately 3 cups licuado)

NUTTY PINEAPPLE SHAKE

PER SERVING:
134 calories
7 g protein
21 g carbohydrate
3 g fat
3 mg cholesterol
103 mg sodium

This is my own idea of what a healthy licuado should be when you want it to take the place of breakfast. One of the great flavor combinations of all time is peanut butter and banana sandwiches ;the next best thing to do is what a health spa in Napa Valley does —blend a tiny bit of nut butter into a fruit drink.

1 cup diced fresh pineapple
1/2 cup sliced banana
2 cups nonfat milk
1/2 cup nonfat yogurt
1 tablespoon almond butter (or peanut butter)
1 teaspoon vanilla
2 teaspoons honey
4 ice cubes

Place all of the ingredients into a blender jar and blend into a frothy shake. If you place the fruit (pineapple and banana slices) into a zip-loc bag the night before and freeze, the shake will be even frothier. This is a creamy, wonderful shake that is so good you will think it is loaded with calories.

Makes 32 ounces or 4 servings, 8 ounces each.

STRAWBERRIES AND CREAM LICUADO

This licuado is not really strawberries and cream but just tastes like it. Kids love this one.

1 cup fresh strawberries, sliced
1 cup low-fat milk (2%)
1/4 cup nonfat yogurt
1/2 teaspoon pure vanilla extract
3 teaspoons sugar (or honey)
4 ice cubes

Place everything in a blender jar and puree until frothy. You can substitute peaches, blueberries, or any particularly sweet fruit in season in exchange for the strawberries. You may also use frozen fruit which will make the drink even frothier.

2 servings. Makes 16 ounces.

STRAWBERRY ORANGE LICUADO

When I lived in San Miguel de Allende, spring always meant the coming of the small strawberries and the sweet, spindly asparagus. The vendor walked down the narrow, cobbled streets in the morning, yelling, "Fresas, Asparaaaaaagus!" I could never resist his cry. From the wooden tray hanging around his neck he would let me have my pick.

1 cup sliced strawberries
1 cup fresh orange juice
4 ice cubes

Place all of the ingredients in a blender jar and puree until frothy.

2 servings or about 3 cups.

AGUA FRESA DE SANDÍA
WATERMELON JUICE

A great deal is lost in the translation of agua fresca de sandía to watermelon juice. It is not simply juice. In Mexico, whether you are passing a Sunday in Chapultepec Park or on a street corner in a small village, you are often confronted with the huge glass barrels sparkling with all colors of various fruit aguas; my favorite is watermelon, a Mexican hot pink juice that when served over shaved ice and eaten with a taco is a small piece of heaven.

PER SERVING:
45 calories
.7 g protein
10 g carbohydrate
.5 g fat
0 mg cholesterol
2 mg sodium

Frequently, when I have had a summer barbecue, the agua fresca of watermelon is gone before the beer. Many traditional methods of preparing aguas fresas load up with sugar. The recipe below, if prepared with sweet watermelon, does not require as much sugar.

6 cups diced watermelon
1 tablespoon reserved seeds
2 cups water
1 tablespoon sugar
Juice from 1 lime, about 1 and 1/2 tablespoons juice
Lime wedges cut from 2 limes for garnish
Chopped or shaved ice

Puree half the amount of watermelon with 1 cup of water. Pour into a pretty glass pitcher and then add the rest of the fruit, water, lime juice, and sugar to the blender and puree. Add this to the juice in the pitcher and then stir in the reserved seeds to make an aguas fresas properly Mexican.

Pour over shaved ice in clear glasses and garnish with a wedge of lime.

8 servings although 4 people usually drink it all!

JAMAICA

One of the most traditional, old-fashioned drinks served by Mexicans, jamaica is an infusion or tea made of steeped dried hibiscus flowers. It is usually served cold or over ice for fiestas. It is tart like cranberry juice so it is always sweetened heavily with sugar. If it is made less strong, it does not require all the sweetening and it is still a pretty raspberry red.

4 ounces dried hibiscus flowers
1 quart hot water
1/4 cup sugar
1 quart cold water
12 ounces frozen apple juice concentrate (1 large can)

Using a heat-proof pitcher (not plastic) or a tea pot, pour the quart of boiling water over the flowers and steep for 10 to 15 minutes.

Pour through a strainer to remove flowers. Be cautious about spilling for the liquid is a staining bright red. It is best to use 2 2-quart pitchers for the mixing, dividing the liquid in half. Add sugar to the warm liquid and stir until dissolved. Then add the cold water. Blend in the frozen apple juice concentrate. This amount is just enough to sweeten the jamaica (without so much sugar) and yet not dominate the drink.

Makes 3 quarts or about 12 servings

PER SERVING:
75 calories
.7 g protein
10 g carbohydrate
.5 g fat
0 mg cholesterol
2 mg sodium

INDULGENCES

CHAPTER VII

FRUIT DESSERTS AND CHOCOLATE

ven though many of us can speak in a very intelligent, even learned fashion about nutrition and proper diets, when given the chance we are as eager as children for a treat or an indulgence. We all know that our everyday dessert mainstay should be fruit or a cup of French roast coffee served in a beautiful cup. If you save up for desserts, they will taste even better.

Except for holidays or birthdays, my California rancho family, with its strong Spanish traditions, never served dessert except fresh fruit usually picked off a nearby tree. A gigantic bowl of apples, peaches, figs, apricots, or grapes was placed on the table. You were given a small plate and a knife to peel and cut your fruit. The eating of fruit was ceremonious accompanied by lazy after dinner talk.

If I spot a basket of fresh raspberries in the market, I often splurge on them. Inevitably while waiting in line, someone asks how I can spend so much on a little basket of berries. A fitting reply is to look at their $3 bag of cookies. Treat yourself to things that are good for you whether it be fresh raspberries, or figs, or the summer's first white peaches.

When we speak of fruit for a treat, make it very special and exotic on occasion. Serve fruit in a fanciful way for guests. I do not have the patience for tempering chocolate so I just melt a good brand of semisweet chocolate. Dip whole strawberries into the warm chocolate and lay them on a bed of crushed ice. Turn over once. Do this no more than 30 minutes before serving but hide them!

Of course, when you do splurge on dessert, eat something wonderful rather than ordinary. Left from childhood, is my penchant for graham crackers and I adore anything chocolate. Every six months I allow myself to send for a box of Cafe Beaujolais' (see Note) graham crackers dipped in Belgian bittersweet chocolate. The ritual for my indulgence never varies. Unless I cheat and eat two crackers.

I rinse off a crystal goblet in cold water and place it in the freezer to chill for at least an hour. One chocolate cracker sits waiting on a little plate. I remove the frosty goblet and fill it with nonfat milk (don't laugh!) and quickly rush it to the table where the cracker awaits. One bite of chocolate. One deep swallow of incredibly cold milk and so on. This splurge counts.

POACHED PEARS WITH AMARETTI FILLING

Poaching, when done gently and quickly, is a particularly fine way to treat pears. They remain crisp and by reducing some of the poaching liquid, you have a ready-made sauce. The filling is light and slim and tastes as though you labored for hours. The trick is to use the Dicamillo amaretti cookies (see Resources), which are some of the best.

6 Bartlett pears (do not remove skins)
3 cups of red wine like Burgundy
2 cups water
1/2 cup frozen apple juice concentrate
3/4 cup sugar
2 teaspoons cinnamon
4 cloves
1 cinnamon stick
For filling:
3/4 cup part-skim milk ricotta
2 tablespoons light cream cheese
2 tablespoons powdered sugar
1 teaspoon vanilla
4 amaretti cookies, crushed to a powder
Cinnamon powder for sprinkling
Mint leaves for garnish

PER SERVING:
327 calories
5 g protein
70 g carbohydrate
5 g fat
13 mg cholesterol
87 mg sodium

Wash the pears well. From the bottom of each pear, use a paring knife to cut out a small cavity, including most of core. You only need to remove about 1 tablespoon of pear meat.

In a 3-quart pot, place the wine, water, apple juice concentrate, sugar, cinnamon, cloves, and cinnamon stick. Bring to a simmer and add the pears. Simmer for 12 minutes with lid partially on. Turn the pears every couple of minutes.

Remove the pears to a deep dish. Pour out half of the liquid and discard. Reduce the remaining liquid on medium heat for 15 minutes to concentrate to 1 and 1/2 cups wine syrup. Pour over pears.

For filling, add ricotta, cream cheese, powdered sugar, and vanilla to bowl of food processor and process until smooth and creamy. Place cookies between folded sheet of wax paper. Crush by moving a rolling pin back and forth. This works better than spinning in the food processor. Add the cookie crumbs to the rest of the filling and blend.

Spoon about a tablespoon of filling into the cavity of each pear. Place standing up on dessert plates and spoon about 3 tablespoons of wine syrup over each pear, sprinkle with cinnamon, and add a mint leaf to each stem.

6 servings

APPLE BLUEBERRY CRISP

Cobblers and crisps usually have a great deal of butter but this one is quite delicious with an absolute minimum of fat. It was inspired by a crisp made by Chef David del Nagro at The Oaks Spa in Ojai, California.

1 package frozen blueberries, 16 ounces
1 quart cored, chopped apples (about 3 large)
2 teaspoons cinnamon
2 tablespoon brown sugar
1/2 cup frozen apple juice concentrate
2 teaspoons arrowroot for thickener
1 cup rolled oats
1/2 cup finely ground graham crackers
2 tablespoons brown sugar
2 tablespoons melted corn oil margarine
1 tablespoon frozen apple juice concentrate, thawed

Combine the blueberries, chopped apples, cinnamon, and brown sugar. In a microwave on high power, heat the apple juice concentrate and the arrowroot for 70 seconds until thickened. Blend with a fork or small whisk about halfway through the cooking. Add the thickened juice to the mixed fruit.

For the topping, combine the oats, graham crackers, brown sugar, melted margarine, and thawed apple juice concentrate. Stir together until well-blended.

Pour fruit into a 13" x 7 and 1/2" baking dish. Sprinkle crumbs over the top. Bake in a preheated 350 degree oven for 40 minutes.

8 servings

PER SERVING:
218 calories
26 g protein
43 g carbohydrate
5 g fat
0 mg cholesterol
86 mg sodium

STRAWBERRY MERINGUE SHORTCAKES

PER SERVING:
186 calories
3 g protein
36 g carbohydrate
4 g fat
13 mg cholesterol
65 mg sodium

These cakes are not the regular dry, crisp meringues but bear a resemblance to the Pavlova, the national dessert of Australia.

The centers of these special meringues are soft and creamy, a perfect foil for unsweetened strawberries (peaches are also delicious here).

6 egg whites, room temperature
1/8 teaspoon salt
1 and 1/2 cups sugar (superfine is best)
1 tablespoon cider vinegar
2 teaspoons vanilla extract
1 quart of sliced strawberries
1/2 cup whipping cream
1 tablespoon powdered sugar
1 teaspoon vanilla extract

Note: if you are concerned about using real whipped cream, you could substitute imitation whipped topping.

Using the whisk attachment of an electric mixer, beat the egg whites and salt until soft peaks form. Begin adding the sugar by the tablespoon. Add about 1 tablespoon every 30 seconds. After half of the sugar has been added, add the vanilla. Continue with the sugar additions and then whip in the vinegar. The mixture will be very stiff.

On 2 baking sheets lined with baking parchment, place 10 dollops of meringue. Smooth them out into 4 and 1/2 inch circles.

Bake in a preheated 250 degree oven for only 40 minutes. The meringue shortcakes should remain pale white and soft in the center with a thin crisp shell on the outside. Make sure that your oven is not hotter than 250 degrees. Remove the meringues from the oven and leave them on the baking sheets to cool.

Just before serving time, whip the cream with the powdered sugar and vanilla just until soft peaks form. Spoon 1/2 cup of strawberries over each meringue shortcake, spooning on a tablespoon of whipped cream. If you think you would like to be more generous with the cream, you'll have to double the amount given above but this amount is not included in the nutritional analysis.

10 servings

STRAWBERRY BROWNIE PIZZA

PER SERVING:
247 calories
5 g protein
29 g carbohydrate
14 g fat
66 mg cholesterol
244 mg sodium

Three of these brownie pizzas at the opening of an art exhibit were swamped immediately and gone within minutes. These are not exactly low-calorie but neither are they decadent when ranked in the dessert hierarchy. Save for special occasions like when you have a lot of mouths to feed.

1/2 cup melted butter
2 eggs
1/2 cup brown sugar
1/4 cup sugar
2 teaspoons vanilla
3/4 cup sweet ground chocolate (Ghiradelli)
1/4 teaspoon salt
2/3 cup unsifted flour
8 ounces light cream cheese, softened
1/4 cup powdered sugar
1 teaspoon vanilla extract
10 strawberries
1/4 cup semisweet chocolate chips, melted

Cut a piece of parchment to fit a 12-inch pizza pan and preheat oven to 350 degrees. This makes it easier to move the giant brownie onto a serving dish later.

Beat the eggs one at a time into the melted butter (or use margarine if you like), next add the brown sugar and regular sugar. Beat well to blend. Then add the vanilla, the ground chocolate, salt, and flour. If you do not have Ghiradelli chocolate, substitute 1/2 cup ground bitter cocoa and 1/4 cup powdered sugar. Mix everything together but do not overblend.

Pour brownie batter out onto the pizza pan and spread to the edges. Bake for approximately 14 minutes. Remove from oven and allow the brownie to cool on the pan. When cool, slide brownie pizza onto flat serving dish or tray.

Beat the cream cheese, powdered sugar, and vanilla together. Spread over the brownie pizza. Slice the strawberries from top to bottom. Arrange in pinwheel fashion around the brownie, starting with the pointed ends of the strawberries facing outward. When the brownie pizza is covered with strawberries, drizzle the melted chocolate artistically over the surface. Cut into wedges to serve.

12 servings

DEVILISH ANGEL FOOD

We have been told over and over that angel food cake is one of the best desserts we can eat because it has no fat. This revelation has brought a lot of old dusty pans out of the back of the cupboard.

But to my way of thinking angel food is only good when its chocolate. I also add Mexican cinnamon, canela, and good expresso powder just so the chocolate tastes more chocolaty.

PER SERVING:
226 calories
7 g protein
49 g carbohydrate
1 g fat
0 mg cholesterol
258 mg sodium

3/4 cup sifted cake flour
1 and 1/2 cups sugar (superfine is preferable)
1/2 cup unsweetened cocoa powder (Dutch-process)
1/2 teaspoon canela
1/2 teaspoon salt
12 egg whites, room temperature
1/2 teaspoon cream of tartar
1 tablespoon instant expresso powder
3 tablespoons warm water
3 teaspoons pure vanilla extract
1 tablespoon powdered sugar
Nonstick angel food cake pan with removable bottom

Preheat oven to 300 degrees. Sift cake flour, 1 cup sugar, cocoa, cinnamon, and salt together three times.

Beat egg whites and cream of tartar using a whip attachment on your mixer. When whites are foamy, begin slowly adding the rest of the sugar, 1/2 cup. Beat to soft peaks. No stiff peaks. Sift flour-cocoa mixture into the egg whites 1/4 cup at a time, folding after each addition. Make sure there are no streaks of flour remaining in the batter.

Combine expresso powder, warm water, and vanilla. Fold into above batter.Spoon batter into an ungreased 10-inch angel food cake pan.

Bake for 50 minutes. Cake should spring back when lightly touched. Remove from oven and invert. Let cake cool completely. Go around the sides with a thin knife and push up removable bottom. Release cake. Place on pretty platter and dust with powdered sugar. Serve as is or with fresh strawberries.

INNOCENT CHOCOLATE SOUFFLE

How could something so innocent taste this good? Try it and you will be amazed.

2 teaspoons butter for coating souffle dish
2 teaspoons superfine sugar
2 tablespoons arrowroot powder
1 and 1/2 teaspoons instant expresso powder
 (Medaglia D'Oro is great)
4 tablespoons superfine sugar
6 tablespoons cocoa powder
    (Dutch-process or Italian)
1 cup nonfat milk
2 teaspoons pure vanilla
5 egg whites
1/2 teaspoon cream of tartar
1/2 cup superfine sugar
1-quart size souffle dish

PER SERVING:
257 calories
8 g protein
51 g carbohydrate
3 g fat
6 mg cholesterol
178 mg sodium

Preheat oven to 375 degrees. Coat the souffle dish with butter. Dust with the 2 teaspoons sugar so the inside of the dish is completely coated. This will help create a marvelous crust.

Combine arrowroot, powdered expresso, 4 tablespoons sugar, cocoa, and the nonfat milk. Heat at 90 power in microwave oven for about 140 seconds. Whisk mixture. It will be very thick and will be the base for your souffle. Whisk in the vanilla. Alternatively, you can whisk the mixture in a small saucepan on your stove.

Beat whites until foamy. Add cream of tartar. Beat until soft peaks form and then slowly add the 1/2 cup sugar. Beat until stiff but not dry. Stir a quarter of the beaten whites into the chocolate mixture. Then fold the lightened chocolate into the remaining beaten whites. Gently spoon into souffle dish and place in a roasting pan. Add an inch of hot water to the roasting pan to create a baño de Maria. Bake about 28 minutes. Top should feel firm. The souffle has a crusty top and soft interior. Serve IMMEDIATELY to 4 waiting people or one husband on Valentine's Day.

NORMA'S ELEGANT PERSIMMON

In every book I have done, my dear friend Norma has one of her best recipes, kind of like breaking a bottle of champagne over the ship's prow before the maiden voyage. She only eats dessert if it is fruit or if it is uncommonly good so I trust her greatly.

1 perfectly ripe persimmon
2 tablespoons good brandy or Grand Marnier

Freeze persimmon for several hours.

Just 20 minutes before serving, slice persimmon in paper thin pieces using a serrated knife. Hopefully, the fruit should still be crystalline. Place on a dessert plate and drizzle with the Grand Marnier. Serve immediately because you want it to taste like persimmon sorbet.

Serves 1. If you need more, freeze 1 persimmon per person.

FRESH FRUIT IN VANILLA SYRUP

I wanted to end with a simple pleasure, a recipe that is one of my daily standbys.

1 cup water
1 cup sugar
1 4-inch piece vanilla bean, split
3 cups of assorted fruit: sliced peaches, sliced straw-
    berries, halved, seedless grapes, mango, and ba-
    nana

Simmer the water, sugar, and vanilla bean (I scrape it to release the heart of the vanilla) for 10 minutes.

Cool the vanilla syrup down just until it is warm to the touch. Pour it over the fruit and let the flavor soak in for at least 1 hour before serving.

PER SERVING:
179 calories
0 g protein
45 g carbohydrate
0 g fat
0 mg cholesterol
0 mg sodium

Note: I keep a bottle of vanilla syrup in the refrigerator to add to quick bowls of fruit.

INDEX

Almonds
  Almond butter, 179
  Grape Salsa, 42
Amaretti cookies
  Poached Pears with, 187
Anaheim chiles
  Albóndigas, 93
  Chili Bouillabaisse, 112
  Chiles Rellenos, 19
  Chiles Stuffed With Corn and Zucchini, 25
  Corn Enchiladas, 142
  Enchiladas Verdes, 165
  Green Chile Stew, 152
  Green Corn Tamales, 142
  Jacquie's Everyday Salsa, 172
  Santa Fe Stroganoff, 156
  Sopa de Maíz, 100
  Rancho Colache, 138
  Turkey Green Chile Stew, 155
  White Bean Chili, 127
Anasazi beans
  Basic Simple Beans, 121
  Dynamite Vegetarian Chili, 119
Ancho chiles
  Black Bean Chili, 122
  Killer Red Sauce, 159
  30-Minute Pozole, 26
  Toasted Sopa de Tortilla, 90
Appetizers
  Black Bean Dip, 65
  Jalapeño Carrots, 48
  Marinated Jicama Sticks, 64
  Red Pepper Cilantro Pesto Torte, 62
  Skinny Guacamole, 64

  Tortilla Turkey Roll-Ups, 66
Apples
  Apple Blueberry Crisp, 189
  Red Cabbage and Apple Salad, 59
Apple juice
  Jamaica, 183,
  with poached pears, 187
Asiago cheese
  Cilantro Pesto, 62
Atole cornmeal
  Banana Blue Corn Muffins, 149
Avocados
  Caldo de Tlapeño, 82
  Grapefruit, Orange, and Avocado Salad, 57
  Guacamole Dressing, 49
  Hacked-Up Salsa, 172
  Skinny Guacamole, 64
  The Best Chicken Tostada Salad, 43
  Toasted Sopa de Tortilla, 90
  Turkey Breast Green Chile Stew, 155
Bananas
  Blue Corn Banana Muffins, 149
  Nutty Pineapple Shake, 179
  San Miguel Market Licuado, 178
Barbecue
  Baja California Fish Tacos, 106
  Grilled Yucatán Fish, 105
Barley
  Black Bean Pancakes, 124
  Steamed Barley, 124
Beans
  Arroz Negro, 17
  Basic Simple Beans, 121

Black Bean Chili, 122
Black Bean Seafood Chili, 114
Black Beans for Salads, 45
Black Bean Pancakes, 124
Black Bean Soup, 96
Dynamite Vegetarian Chili, 119
Enchilada Soup, 84
Mexican Minestrone, 78
Navaho Bean Salad, 126
Tarascan Soup, 94
The Best Beans, 16
The Best Chicken Tostada Salad, 43
Thickened Beans (like refried), 16
White Bean Chili, 129

Beef
Albóndigas (Meatballs), 93
Santa Fe Stroganoff, 156
Taco Salad with Salsa Dressing, 46

Beer
Chicken Chili, 147
Turkey Tenderloins, 168

Black Beans, see Beans

Blueberry
Apple Blueberry Crisp, 189

Blue Cheese
Pear Salad, 56

Blue Corn
Banana Blue Corn Muffins, 149

Breads
Healthy Flour Tortillas, 33
Banana Blue Corn Muffins, 149

Breadcrumbs
Chiles Rellenos, 19
Salsa Chicken, 35
Albóndigas, 93

Brownies
Strawberry Brownie Pizza, 192

Brown Rice
Brown Rice Lentil Salad, 139
Janet's Chicken Soup, 74

Bulgur
Dynamite Vegetarian Chili, 119

Burrito
Vegetable Burritos With Killer Red Sauce, 158

Cabbage
Mexican Coleslaw, 59
Mexican Minestrone, 78
Red Cabbage and Apple Salad, 59

Cactus (Nopalitos)
Navaho Bean Salad, 126

Cake
Devilish Angel Food, 193

Carrots
Grandma's Rice, 18
Green Chile Stew, 152
Jalapeño Carrots, 48
Janet's Chicken Soup, 74
Lentil Chili, 128
Mexican Minestrone, 78
Mexican Vegetable Soup, 92

Cheese
Black Bean Chili Au Gratin, 122
Chiles Rellenos, 19
Corn Enchiladas, 142
Eggplant Enchiladas, 164
Enchiladas Verdes, 165
Inside Out Quesadilla, 173
Marinated Chiles Rellenos, 21
Mexican Minestrone with Cilantro Pesto, 78
Red Pepper Cilantro Pesto Torte, 62
Stacked Onion-Cheese Enchiladas, 29
Vegetable Burrito With Killer Red Sauce, 158
Spicy Split Pea Soup, 87

Chicken
Caldo de Tlapeño, 82
Chicken Chili, 147
Chicken Rapído, 170
Chicken Tostada with Grape Salsa, 42
Chicken Colorado, 161
Enchiladas Verdes, 165
Janet's Chicken Soup, 74
Pan de Maíz, 146
Poblano Chiles Stuffed
  With Fruit and Chicken, 23

Posole, 132
Salsa Chicken, 35
Soft Tacos, 171
The Best Chicken Tostada, 43
White Bean Chili, 29
Chicken Broth
Fearless Chicken Broth, 71
Friendly Chicken Broth, 72
Chile Sauce
Killer Red Sauce, 159
Red Chile and Roasted Garlic Sauce, 28
Chili
Black Bean Chili, 122
Black Bean Seafood Chili, 114
Bouillabaisse Chili, 112
Chicken Chili, 147
Dynamite Vegetarian Chili, 119
Lentil Chili, 128
White Bean Chili, 129
Chipotle Chile
Baja California Fish Tacos, 106
Best Beans, 16
Black Bean Chili Au Gratin, 122
Black Bean Seafood Chili, 114
Grilled Yucatán Fish, 105
Smoked Fire Salsa, 175
Turkey Breast Chorizo, 30
Turkey Chipotle Tostada, 40
Chocolate
Devilish Angel Food, 193
Innocent Chocolate Souffle, 195
Strawberry Brownie Pizza, 192
Corn
Best Chicken Tostada Salad, 43
Corn-Brown Rice-Lentil Salad, 139
Chicken Chili, 147
Chiles Stuffed with Corn and Zucchini, 25
Corn Enchiladas, 142
Dynamite Vegetarian Chili, 119
Green Corn Tamales, 144
Mexican Vegetable Soup, 92

New Mexican Potato Salad, 34
Pan de Maíz, 146
Rancho Colache, 138
Sopa de Maíz, 100
Tamale Pie, 136
Cornmeal
Black Bean Pancakes, 124
Green Corn Tamales, 144
Pan de Maíz, 146
Tamale Pie, 136
Cucumbers
Basque Salad, 55
Easy Mexican Gazpacho, 98
Eggs
Jose's Special, 32
Eggplant
Eggplant Enchiladas, 164
Enchiladas
Corn Enchiladas, 142
Eggplant Enchiladas, 164
Enchiladas Verdes, 165
Stacked Onion and Cheese, 29
Enchiladas of the Jardín, 162
Grapes
Grape Salsa, 42
Grapenuts
Apple Blueberry Crisp, 189
Green Beans
Navaho Bean Salad, 126
Mexican Vegetable Salsa Soup, 92
Green Chiles (see Anaheim Chiles)
Ham
Basic Simple Beans, 121
Black Bean Soup, 96
Hibiscus Flowers (Dried for Tea)
Jamaica, 183
Jalapeño Chile
Black Bean Dip, 65
Cream Cheese Filling, 22
Dynamite Vegetarian Chili, 119
Fast Tomatillo Salsa, 167

Green Chile Stew, 152
Hacked-up Salsa, 172
Jacquie's Everyday Salsa, 172
Jalapeño Carrots, 48
Jalapeño Vinaigrette, 141
Lucy's Hot Salsa, 107
Mexican Coleslaw, 59
Salsa Fresca with Spaghetti, 52
Sweet Potato Jalapeño Soup, 88
Tortilla Turkey Roll-ups, 66
Jamaica Tea, 183
Jicama
Jicama and Red Pepper Salad, 54
Lentil Chili, 128
Marinated Jicama Sticks, 64
Kale
Mexican Minestrone, 78
Lemon
Janet's Chicken Soup, 74
Marinated Jicama Sticks, 64
Skinny Guacamole, 64
Lentils
Brown Rice Lentil Salad, 139
Lentil Chili, 128
Limes
Ceviche Salad, 109
Hacked-Up Salsa, 172
Marinade for Fish Tacos, 106
Sopa de Lima, 76
Yucatán Grilled Fish, 105
Watermelon Juice, 181
Meats, see Beef, Chicken, or Turkey
Muffins
Blue Corn Banana Muffins, 149
Mushrooms
Santa Fe Stroganoff, 156
Mussels
Chili Bouillabaisse Chili, 112
New Mexican Chiles
Black Bean Chili,122
Chicken Chili,147

Chicken Colorado, 161
Chiles Rellenos, 19
Corn Enchiladas, 142
Dynamite Vegetarian Chili, 119
Killer Red Sauce, 159
Marinated Chiles Rellenos, 21
Posole, 132
Red Chile and Roasted Garlic Sauce, 28
Stacked Onion and Cheese Enchiladas, 27
Oatmeal
Apple Blueberry Crisp, 189
Olives
Chicken Chili, 147
Enchilada Soup, 84
New Mexican Potato Salad, 60
Red Snapper Filets, 110
Tamale Pie, 136
Tortilla Turkey Roll-ups, 66
Onions
Pink Pickled Onions, 41
Oranges
Grapefruit-Orange Avocado- Salad, 57
Orange Juice
Ceviche Salad, 109
Grilled Yucatán Fish, 105
San Miguel Market Licuado, 178
Strawberry Orange Licuado, 180
Pancakes
Black Bean Pancakes, 124
Pasta
Mexican Minestrone, 78
Mexican Vegetable Soup, 92
Sopa de Fideos, 81
Spaghetti Salad with Salsa, 52
Peaches
Fresh Fruit in Vanilla Syrup, 197
Poblano Chiles Stuffed With Fruit
  and Chicken, 23
Pears
Pear Salad, 56
Poached Pears With Amaretti, 187

Peas
 Grandma's Rice, 18
 Spicy Split Pea Soup, 87
Pecans
 Red Cabbage Apple Salad, 59
Persimmons
 Norma's Elegant Persimmon, 196
Pesto
 Mexican Minestrone with Cilantro Pesto, 78
 Red Pepper Cilantro Pesto Torte, 62
Pineapple
 Nutty Pineapple Shake, 179
 San Miguel Market Licuado, 178
Pinto Beans
 Basic Simple Beans, 121
 Dynamite Vegetarian Chili, 119
 Mexican Minestrone, 78
 Navaho Bean Salad, 126
 Tarascan Bean Soup, 94
Poblano Chiles
 Poblano Chiles Stuffed With Fruit
  and Chicken, 23
Poppy seeds
 Poppy seed Dressing, 57
Pork
 Green Chile Stew, 152
 Posole, 132
Posole (Hulled Corn Kernels)
 About, 131
 Posole, 132
Potatoes
 Caldo de Tlalpeño, 82
 Green Chile Stew, 152
 Mexican Vegetable Soup, 92
 New Mexican Potato Salad, 60
 Sopa de Maíz, 100
Raisins
 Poblano Chiles Stuffed With Fruit
  and Chicken, 23
 Red Cabbage and Apple Salad, 59
 Tamale Pie, 136
Red Chiles (Dried)
 Black Bean Soup, 96
 Corn Enchiladas, 142
 Enchilada Soup, 84
 Killer Red Sauce, 159
 Posole, 132
 Red Chile and Roasted Garlic Sauce, 28
 Tarascan Bean Soup, 94
 Toasted Sopa de Tortilla, 90
Red (Bell) Peppers
 Dynamite Vegetarian Chili, 119
 Red Pepper Cilantro Pesto Torte, 62
 Red Pepper Sauce, 168
 Sopa de Maíz, 100
Red Snapper (Fish)
 Baja Fish Tacos, 106
 Bouillabaisse Chili, 112
 Grilled Yucatán Fish, 105
 Red Snapper Veracruz Style, 110
Rice
 Arroz Negro, 17
 Black Bean Soup with, 96
 Brown Rice-Lentil Salad, 139
 Grandma's Rice, 18
 Yellow Rice, 84
Ricotta Cheese
 Red Pepper Cilantro Pesto Torte, 62
 Poached Pears With Amaretti Filling, 187
Romaine Lettuce
 Baja Fish Tacos, 106
 Captains's Caesar Salad, 49
 Chicken Tostada With Grape Salsa, 42
 Taco Salad with Salsa Dressing, 46
 The Best Chicken Tostada, 43
 Turkey Chipotle Tostada, 40
Salads (see individual ingredient listings)
Salad Dressings
 Creamy Mex Dressing, 43
 Guacamole Dressing, 49
 Jalapeño Vinaigrette, 139
 Salsa Dressing, 46
 Salsa Fresca for Spaghetti, 52

Salsas
Jacquie's Everyday Salsa, 172
Grape Salsa, 42
Fast Tomatillo Salsa, 167
Lucy's Hot Salsa, 107
Salsa Fresca with Pasta, 52
Smoked Fire, 175
Quick Fresh Salsa, 23

Scallops
Black Bean Seafood Chili, 114
Bouillabaisse Chili 112
Ceviche Salad, 109

Shrimp
Black Bean Seafood Chili, 114
Bouillabaisse Chili, 112

Sour Cream
Black Bean Pancakes, 124
Enchiladas Verdes, 165
Green Corn Tamales, 144
Santa Fe Stroganoff, 156
Turkey Tenderloins, 149

Spaghetti
Warm Spaghetti Salad With Salsa, 52
Sopa De Fideos (Angel Hair Pasta), 81

Spinach
Hugo's Caldo de Tlapeño, 82
Jose's Special, 32
Mexican Minestrone, 78
Pear Salad, 56

Split Peas
Spicy Split Pea Soup, 87

Squash (Zucchini)
Chiles Stuffed With Corn and Zucchini, 25
Green Corn Tamales, 144
Mexican Minestrone, 78
Rancho Colache, 138
Vegetable Burrito, 158

Strawberries
Fruit Rainbow Licuado, 178
Strawberry Brownie Pizza, 192
Strawberries and Cream Licuado, 180
Strawberry Meringue Shortcakes, 190

Strawberry Orange Licuado, 180
Stews
Green Chile Stew, 152
Posole, 132
Santa Fe Stroganoff, 156
Turkey Green Chile Stew, 155

Sweet Potatoes
Sweet Potato Jalapeño Soup, 88
Turkey Green Chile Stew, 155

Tacos
Baja Fish Tacos, 106
Soft Tacos With Salsas, 171

Tomatillos
Fast Tomatillo Salsa, 167
Jacquie's Everyday Salsa, 172
White Bean Chili, 129

Tomatoes
Black Bean Seafood Chili, 114
Bouillabaisse Chili, 112
Chicken Chili, 147
Dynamite Vegetarian Chili, 119
Easy Mexican Gazpacho, 98
Enchilada Soup, 84
Grandma's Rice, 18
Hacked-Up Salsa, 172
Lucy's Hot Salsa, 107
Killer Red Sauce, 159
Lentil Chili, 128
Mexican Minestrone, 78
Mexican Vegetable Salsa Soup, 92
Rancho Colache, 138
Red Chile and Roasted Garlic Sauce, 28
Red Snapper Vera Cruz, 110
Salsa Fresca, 52
Smoked Fire, 175
Tarascan Bean Soup, 94
Quick Fresh Salsa, 23

Tortillas
Healthy Flour Tortillas, 33

Tostadas
Chicken Tostada With Grape Salsa, 42
The Best Chicken Tostada Salad, 43

Turkey Chipotle Tostada, 40

Tofu
Dynamite Vegetarian Chili, 119

Turkey
Albóndigas (Meatballs), 93
Jose's Special, 32
Lentil Chili, 128
Spicy Turkey Tenderloin 168
Tamale Pie, 136
Turkey Breast Chorizo, 30
Turkey Breast Green Chile Stew, 155
Turkey Chipotle Tostada, 40

Vegetables (see Individual Vegetables)

Walnuts
Pear Salad, 56
Poblano Chiles Stuffed With Fruit and Chicken, 23

Watermelon
Fruit Rainbow Licuado, 178
Watermelon Juice, 181

Wholewheat Flour
Blue Corn Banana Muffins, 149

Yogurt
Blue Corn Banana Muffins, 149
Eggplant Enchiladas, 164
Nutty Pineapple Shake, 179
Strawberry and Cream Licuado, 180
Turkey Chipotle Tostada, 40

RESOURCES

AND OTHER UNUSUAL MEXICAN AND SOUTHWESTERN INGREDIENTS

DON ALFONSO FOODS
P.O. Box 201988Austin, Texas 78720-19881-800-456-6100
Don Alfonso Foods makes delicious chipotles en adobo packed in a glass jar and pureed chipotles en adobo immediately ready for the cook to stir into dishes. Carry tan chipotles, moras, and morita chiles and many of the other unusual chiles from Mexico including all the chiles for authentic mole. Catalog available.

SANTA FE SCHOOL OF COOKING
116 West San Francisco St.Santa Fe, New Mexico 87501 (505) 983-4511 For orders
They carry a wonderful masa harina (dehydrated masa) that I use for tortillas and tamales. The meal is stoneground in Texas and has incomparable flavor compared to supermarket brands. Also have exotic dried beans, dried chiles, and blue corn.They carry both Don Alfonso Chipotles and the new Santafire. Southwestern cooking classes available.

RANCHO MESILLA
P.O. Box 39Mesilla, New Mexico 88046 (505) 525-2266 For orders
Stuart Hudson will air freight New Mexican long green chiles grown along the fertile Rio Grande; chiles are fire-roasted and peel easily;also available are smoky chiles pasados, the dried red New Mexican chiles which are cold-smoked. Hot, sweet, and lighter smoke flavor than Mexican chipotles.

TIERRA VEGETABLE FARM
Healdsburg, California (707) 433-5666 for chile orders
Produce some of the most delicious chipotles I have ever tasted. Ranch-grown chiles are smoke-cured over orchard fruitwood and grapevine cuttings in an outdoor brick oven.

JUST TOMATOES
P.O. Box 807 Westley, California 95387 1-800-537-1985
Intensely sweet, vine-ripened tomatoes dried and packaged by this small company; great in salsas especially in the winter when only pink golf balls are available in supermarkets. Come in thin slices so they reconstitute almost immediately for use in cooking.

ROUND TOP CAFE, THE ROYERS
On the SquareRound Top, Texas 78954 1-800-8GROYERS
This family operation produces a delicious vinegar called Pepper Sauce which I use to spark salsas and salad dressings. Bottles are colorfully packed with red and green jalapeños, cilantro, onions, vinegar, spices, and probably something secret. I bought my first bottle in Macy's in San Francisco and was desperate when I ran out so I called the phone number on the bottle's label and reached Bud at the Round Top Cafe (shades of the Whistle Stop Cafe in "Fried Green Tomatoes"). He chatted up a storm and said,"Sure I'll send you more Pepper Sauce.

PENDERY'S OF TEXAS
1-800-533-1870
Expansive selection of dried herbs, spices, dried chiles, and Mexican ingredients

DICAMILLO BAKERY
811 Linwood Ave.
Niagara Falls, N.Y. 14305
Produce my favorite amaretti cookie.

AIDELL SAUSAGE COMPANY
1575 Minnosota St.
Sn Francisco, Ca.
415-285-6660
Produce homemade-style chorizo, Cajun tasso (great in beans), and other great sausges.

THE CHILE SHOP
505-983-6080
Dixon chile.

BARGETTO SOQUEL WINERY
Soquel, Ca. 95073
Produce fine red and white wine vinegars (90 grain).